Books in Spanish for Children and Young Adults: An Annotated Guide

SERIES II

Libros Infantiles y Juveniles en Español: Una Guía Anotada

SERIE NO. II

by
ISABEL SCHON

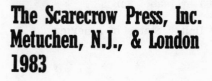
The Scarecrow Press, Inc.
Metuchen, N.J., & London
1983

Library of Congress Cataloging in Publication Data

Schon, Isabel.
    Books in Spanish for children and young adults.

    Includes index.
    1. Children's literature, Spanish—Bibliography.
    2. Children's literature, Spanish American—
    Bibliography. I. Title. II. Title: Libros infantiles
    y juveniles en español. Serie no. II.
    Z2694.5.S35 1983   011'.62   83-3315
    [PQ6168]
    ISBN 0-8108-1620-2

To my parents,
Dr. Oswald Schon
and
Mrs. Anita Schon

to my husband,
Dr. Richard R. Chalquest

to my daughter,
Verita

and to all the young readers
who inspired me

PREFACE

Like its predecessor, this book is intended to serve as a guide to any adult--teacher, librarian, counselor, layman, or parent--who is interested in selecting books in Spanish written by Hispanic authors for children of preschool through high school age. Most of the books included in this guide were published after 1978 and come from Argentina, Chile, Colombia, Costa Rica, Cuba, Ecuador, Mexico, Peru, Puerto Rico, Spain, Uruguay, and Venezuela.

I have identified books for children and young adults that highlight the lifestyle, folklore, heroes, history, fiction, poetry, theatre, and classical literature of Hispanic cultures as expressed by Hispanic authors. Therefore, no translations or textbooks are included. Though such an undertaking is overly ambitious, I have attempted to include most books that are readily available in Spanish-speaking countries and that represent the books that Hispanic young readers are now reading in their own countries. All of the books reviewed were still in print as of October 1982. To assist the selector, I have used the following symbols with each book annotated:

* Asterisks denote outstanding books: entertaining reading with a high potential for reader involvement or interest.

m Marginal books: may be used to supplement a collection; but the book may be difficult to read, may lack attractive illustrations, or may lack reader appeal.

nr Not Recommended: mostly dull books

I have also indicated a tentative grade level for each book, but the individual student's Spanish reading ability, interest, taste, and purpose should be the main criteria for determining the true level of each book.

The selector will also note that a few Spanish-speaking countries are not represented in this book and that Spain and Argentina have the greatest number of books for young readers. This reflects the actual state of the publishing industry for young readers in Spanish-speaking countries. Books are still an expensive luxury in much of Latin America.

To assist selectors in ordering these books, I have included in Appendix I the names and addresses of dealers in Spanish-speaking countries who in my experience will expedite shipment of any order. These dealers are highly recommended for their efficiency and prompt service. I have also included in Appendix II a list of book dealers in the United States who specialize in books from Spanish-speaking countries. Unfortunately, not all of the books recommended in this guide are now available in the United States.

It is my sincere hope that this book will assist all readers in understanding the heritage of Hispanic people and in appreciating the beauty and variety of Hispanic customs through the writings of Hispanic authors.

I wish to express my appreciation to my husband, Dr. R. R. Chalquest, for his patience and encouragement; to the many librarians in the Spanish-speaking countries for their gracious cooperation; to the Department of Educational Technology and Library Science, Arizona State University, for its support; to the professional staff of the University Library, Arizona State University, for their continued assistance; and to Mrs. Elizabeth Outcalt for her marvelous cooperation.

Isabel Schon, Ph. D.
Associate Professor in Library Science
Arizona State University, Tempe
October 1982

PROLOGO

Así como su predecesor, la intención de este libro es la de servir como guía a cualquier adulto, ya sea profesor, bibliotecario, consejero, o padre, que esté interesado en seleccionar libros en español escritos por autores hispanos para jóvenes de edad preescolar hasta la secundaria. La mayoría de los libros incluidos en este guía han sido publicados después de 1978 en Argentina, Chile, Colombia, Costa Rica, Cuba, Ecuador, México, Perú, Puerto Rico, España, Uruguay, y Venezuela.

He identificado libros infantiles y juveniles que demuestran el estilo de vida, folklore, héroes, historia, ficción, poesía, teatro, y literatura clásica de las culturas hispanas como han sido expresadas por autores hispanos. Por lo tanto, no he incluido traducciones ni libros de texto. Aún cuando mi empresa es demasiado ambiciosa, he tratado de incluir el mayor número de los libros que están disponibles en países hispanos y los libros que leen ahora los jóvenes lectores hispanos en sus propios países. Ninguno de los libros reseñados estaba agotado hasta octubre de 1982. Para ayudar al selector, he usado los siguientes símbolos con cada libro anotado:

* Asteriscos significan libros sobresalientes: lectura divertida con un gran potencial de interesar al lector.

m Libros Mediocres: pueden ser usado para completar una colección pero los libros pueden ser difícil de leer, y ser deficiente en ilustraciones o deficiente en atractivos para el lector.

nr No Recomendables: casi siempre libros aburridos.

También he indicado un grado tentativo de lectura para cada

libro, pero el nivel de lectura de cada lector, así como sus intereses, gustos y propósitos, deben ser los criterios más importantes para determinar el nivel verdadero de cada libro.

El selector también notará que algunos países hispanos no están representados en este libro y que España y Argentina tienen el mayor número de libros para jóvenes lectores. Esto refleja el estado actual de la industria editorial para jóvenes en países hispanos. En mucho de Hispanoamérica libros son todavía un lujo muy caro.

Para ayudar a los selectores en ordenar estos libros, he incluido en el Apéndice I los nombres y direcciónes de negociantes en países hispanos que en mi experiencia apresurarán el envío de cualquier orden. Estos negociantes son eficientes y procuran dar un buen servicio. También he incluido en el Apéndice II una lista de negociantes de libros en los Estados Unidos que se especializan en libros de países hispanos. Desgraciadamente, no todos los libros recomendados en este guía están disponibles ahora en los Estados Unidos.

Mis más sinceros deseos son que este libro ayude a todos los lectores a comprender la herencia cultural, la belleza, y la variedad de costumbres hispanas como han sido expresadas por autores hispanos.

Quisiera expresar mi agradecimiento a mi esposo, Dr. R. R. Chalquest, por su paciencia y apoyo, a los bibliotecarios de todos los países hispanos por su amable ayuda, al Departamento de Tecnología Educativa y Biblioteconomía en Arizona State University por su apoyo, al personal profesional de la biblioteca de Arizona State University por su ayuda, y a la Sra. Elizabeth Outcalt por su amable cooperación.

Dra. Isabel Schon
Profesora en Biblioteconomía
Arizona State University, Tempe
octubre 1982

TABLE OF CONTENTS

x

ARGENTINA

FICTION

m Abalos, Jorge W. Andanzas de Jabutí la tortuguita.
Illus: Carlos Alberto Riolfi. (Buenos Aires: Editorial
Plus Ultra, 1979. 62 p.) Gr. 4-7.

This is a delightful adaptation of an Argentine folk-
tale about the ingenuous adventures of Jabutí, the turtle.
Unfortunately, stale and bland illustrations detract from
the clever adventures in which the turtle is constantly
engaged to defend her life in the jungle: Jabutí, the
turtle, must confront Anta, the tapir; Yaguareté, the
tiger; Cururú, the toad; Guasú, the deer; Micuré, the
weasel; Curupira, the giant; man; and finally Urubú, the
crow. After reading about the amazing undertakings of
Jabutí, young readers will know why the turtle is now so
slow and has a flat chest.

m Amable, Hugo. Tierra encendida de espejos. (Buenos
Aires: Editorial Plus Ultra, 1980. 77 p.) Gr. 10-12.

The author explains that in this collection of twelve
brief short stories his main character is humankind's
work and daily life, joys and sorrows, successes and
frustrations. The first four short stories, which are
grouped under the title "Women in the Mirror of Time,"
are the most interesting to read. They tell of the love
lives of four women: Isabel Yaguareté, the daughter of
a brave Indian chief, who saved the life of the Spanish
adventurer, Alvaro Alonso de Figueroa; Malinche, the
beautiful and intelligent Indian maiden who accompanied
Cortés in his Conquest of Mexico; Lucrecia, the rejected
maiden who married the eternal liar Don García; and the

1

life, love, and death of Georgina Hubner, who was im-
mortalized in Juan Ramón Jiménez' famous elegy "Carta
a Georgina Hubner." Unfortunately, the other stories are
vague condemnations of people's reckless behavior; they
either convey a moral or are abstract mysteries that
describe strange occurrences.

* Arribillaga, Manuelita.   ¡Liralirón! Illus: Leticia
Uhalde. (Buenos Aires: Editorial Plus Ultra, 1978.
47 p.) Gr. 2-4.

Eighteen simple, lively rhymes about things common
to children. It includes rhymes about animals, toys, and
games. The unaffected language used in these rhymes
will certainly appeal to children. Here is an example:

Canción de cuna para mi muñeca

Duérmete muñeca,
duérmete mi amor,
que si tu no duermes
no me duermo yo.

La luna nos mira
por una ventana,
cerremos los ojos
hasta la mañana

[Nursery rhyme for my doll

Sleep my doll,
sleep my love,
if you don't sleep
I won't sleep.

The moon looks at us
through the window
let's close our eyes
until tomorrow] (p. 38)

Unfortunately the illustrations do not do much for each
rhyme; they are merely three-tone lifeless decorations.

m Barbieri, Vincente. El libro de las mil cosas. Illus:
Viviana Barletta. (Buenos Aires: Editorial Plus Ultra,
1979. 239 p.) Gr. 8-12.

This book of "a thousand things" contains many se-
lections of Spanish poetry and contemporary Argentine
poets such as Fernando Luis Bernárdez, Leopoldo Mare-
chal, José Hernández, and Jorge Luis Borges. It also
includes short stories of well-known authors such as Her-
man Melville, Hans Christian Andersen, and Argentine
authors such as Manuel Mujica Lainez, Domingo Faustino
Sarmiento, Benito Lynch, along with many others. In
addition the author has included various games and ex-
periments that might appeal to younger readers. The
selection of reading material in this book is indeed ex-
tensive. However, young adults will be turned off by the
games and childish poems, and children will find the se-
lections of the world's classical literature too difficult to
understand.

m   Belgrano, Margarita. El salón vacío. Illus: Nora
Kohan. (Buenos Aires: Centro Editor de América Latina, 1978. 22 p.) Gr. 3-6.

King Tomás was a wealthy and powerful king. He
lived in a huge palace where he had one room for every
occasion, including an empty room which would fill up
with happiness when the king was sad. He became bored
with all these luxuries and decided to look for something
different. He found a bakery shop which sold delicious
"panqueques" (sweet rolls) and ate five of them. He surprised the owners by telling them that he was the king
and that he would like to spend Tuesdays and Thursdays
at the bakery, while the bakers spent the same days living at the king's palace.

*   _____. Los zapatos voladores. Illus: Chacha.
(Buenos Aires: Centro Editor de América Latina, 1978.
26 p.) Gr. 2-4.

A few people in town saw the "flying shoes." The
next day the news was all over town and nobody went to
work; everybody wanted to see the "flying shoe" that was
trapped on top of the TV antenna of the pharmacist's
house. The governor pleaded with the people to go back
to work and to ignore the story of the "flying shoes."
Meanwhile, firemen presented him with the "flying shoe"
but the governor insisted that it was only a shoe. Amidst
this commotion there appeared a barefooted mailman who

explained that he had thrown his shoes out of the window because he got tired of walking and couldn't afford a bicycle. So everybody contributed towards the mailman's new shoes and bicycle.

The amusing illustrations and light-hearted text will please young readers.

*   Bertolino, Roberto. Ayer. Illus: Alejandro Terrera. (Buenos Aires: Editorial Plus Ultra, 1978, 47 p.) Gr. 5-12.

This is a simple and poetic narrative which describes the author's feelings about why "yesterday" will live forever in his heart. The child-like cover and illustrations might deceive some readers into believing that this is a picture book for young children, but its tender, vague thoughts will have more meaning to older readers. Here is an example: "Había una vez un pedazo, de tiempo que se llamaba Ayer.... Parecía el más grande y el más hermoso del mundo.... Porque uníamos las distancias con recuerdos. [Once upon a time there was a piece of time that was called Yesterday.... It looked like the greatest and the most beautiful one in the world .... Because we united distances with memories.]" pp. 8, 10, 38.

m _____. Hoy. Illus: Alejandro Terrera. (Buenos Aires: Editorial Plus Ultra, 1979, 48 p.) Gr. 7-12.

The illustrations of a boy of approximately eight years old seem a little out of place in his narrative in which the author poetically describes his feelings upon losing his loved one. He remembers her in his walks and when he looks at the moon. He waits for her in every corner; he writes to her a hundred letters; he discovers that everything is different without her; and so forth. The following is an example of one page: "Hoy caminé alrededor del silencio buscando tu voz.... Descubrí que estoy solo. [Today I walked around Silence searching for your voice.... I discovered that I am alone.]" p. 20.

These are simple thoughts sentimentally expressed.

nr Bird, Poldy, ed. Amistad, divino tesoro. (Buenos Aires: Ediciones Orión, 1980. 165 p.) Gr. 7-10.

This book was conceived in homage to friendship, thus fourteen Argentine authors wrote stories that tell how two boys became true friends, how one boy sent friendship notes inside balloons to any boy who would be willing to be his friend, how a cat and a dog became good friends, how two boys learned "to share the magic of friendship," and other stories that convey the message that "a friend is a marvelous world." The editor states that these stories will entice young readers toward good literature; I found them wearisome and unenjoyable.

nr   Boccazzi, Dora A. El arroyito que se fue a pasear. Illus: Mariel Rodríguez. (Buenos Aires: Editorial Plus Ultra, 1981. 47 p.) Gr. 4-6.

This contains nine lethargic stories that tell about a small river that went for a walk, a little chair with wings, two dogs that went to the forest, a little fearful rabbit, a little fat pig, an absent-minded elephant, a thin tree, and a playful seed. The three-tone illustrations are as spiritless as the stories.

m   Bocconi, Alicia. Chiquirriqui cruza la selva misionera. Illus: Alicia Charré. (Buenos Aires: Centro Editor de América Latina, 1978. 24 p.) Gr. 2-4.

Chiquirriqui, a white dog from the city, escapes from his owner and goes to visit a nearby forest. There he is assisted by various animals and is given food and a place to sleep; he is also told that man is the forest's enemy because he steals the land and burns the trees. When Chiquirriqui hurts his foot, he is flown back home by his friends, the birds. Long, involved text makes this a difficult story to enjoy.

nr   Bornemann, Elsa Isabel. Bilembambudín. Illus: Guido Bruneris. (Buenos Aires: Ediciones Librerías Fausto, 1979. 128 p.) Gr. 5-8.

A nine-year-old girl relates her fantastic experiences after attending a show with her aunt and uncle where a magician performs various acts of magic. There she was invited to go on a dragon ride to the faraway kingdom of Bilembambudín where she meets Osofronio, a ghost; Doña Naturalia, a witch; two giants who were the king's guards; a man of fire and many other fanciful characters. The story concludes with the author's message to young readers: "No hay talismán mágico que valga, si quien se lo cuelga no se empeña en conseguir sus objetivos a pura fuerza de amor y de trabajo" (p. 124). This unnecessary reminder to love and to work and the long text make this story too complicated for young readers; the black-and-white line illustrations, which are child-like and appealing, are the only redeeming quality of this book.

m _____ . El niño envuelto. (Buenos Aires: Ediciones Orión, 1981. 174 p.) Gr. 6-9.

Andrés, a young boy, tells in a series of brief episodes his experiences as he grows up and discovers the world around him. His first concern was finding out how he was born: His grandmother told him that he was found inside a cabbage; his aunt told him that he was delivered by a stork; but his mother explained that he was the son of the love of his father and mother and how he was formed inside her body. Other episodes tell about his wishes to own a pet, the death of his grandfather, adopting children, his days in school, and other issues that concern him. Some of the episodes are charming and fun to read; others are a little slow and dull.

nr Bressano de Alonso, Olga. La abejita hacendosa y otros cuentos. (Buenos Aires: Editorial Guadalupe, 1978. 95 p.) Gr. 3-6.

These stories pretend to present "scientific truth" through "games and fiction." The result is a tedious collection of nine stories which supposedly narrate the life of various insects: a diligent bee, a happy ant, a useless drone, a dirty fly, a proud flea, a vain dragonfly, a wise cricket, an assembly of spiders, and a motherly tarantula. The elaborate descriptions and moralistic admonitions make these stories neither entertaining nor informative reading.

nr Burgos, Alfredo Pedro. Cuento de cuentos. Illus: Pollini. (Buenos Aires: Editorial Plus Ultra, 1981. 127 p.) Gr. 6-8.

These twenty-nine bland stories are supposed to give young readers "beautiful lessons from nature. " It includes stories about a kind angel, an abandoned toy, the strings of a guitar, a wooden horse, friendship, and others. I wonder why some adults think that young readers will be entertained by lethargic lessons in morality.

nr   Cáceres, Germán. Cuentos para mocosos y purretes. Illus: Luis Pereyra. (Buenos Aires: Editorial Santiago Rueda, 1980. 71 p.) Gr. 2-4.

This is a collection of fourteen absurd stories that will bore children because of their long descriptions and saccharine messages. They tell of happy animals that love to help others, of a kangaroo that became a kind boxer, of fireflies that voted against war, and other dull stories. The following is an example of this author's affected writing style: "Guardián conoció entonces la felicidad. ¡Qué mejor amistad que la de los animales del circo! ¡Y qué mayor satisfacción que ver brillar la alegría en los ojitos de los niños! [Then Guardián knew happiness. What better friendship than that of animals at the circus! And what greater satisfaction than to see the happiness in the little eyes of children!]" p. 20.

m   Calny, Eugenia. El congreso de los árboles. (Buenos Aires: Editorial Plus Ultra, 1979. 183 p.) Gr. 9-12.

The author's purpose in writing this book, which includes thirty-nine brief legends and stories about trees, is to teach young readers that "trees are beauty, friendship, life. To learn to protect and respect them is one of the most delicate forms of love. " Therefore, all the characters with the exception of one boy are trees from all over the world who get together "to remind man that it is necessary to care for them and protect them. " The constant moralizing is obviously tedious reading; however, the brief anecdotes and stories about each tree do make interesting reading. For example, there are amusing stories about the origins of palm trees, trees from Japan, cedar trees, trees from Mexico, olive trees, and many other species.

nr   _____. Gato Rayado y ratoncito lector. Illus: Luis

Pollini.   (Buenos Aires: Editorial Plus Ultra, 1981.
47 p.)   Gr. 4-6.

This book contains nine absurd stories about Don
Rayado, a cat, who does not wish to pursue Ratoncito,
a little mouse.   Ratoncito loved to read at home, because
"he wanted to learn many things. "   Don Rayado was an
excellent cook and loved to cook for his friends.   Other
stories show Don Rayado learning to play the guitar and
reading the telephone directory.   The long text and childish illustrations will not appeal to fourth-sixth graders.

nr _____.   La gaviota perdida.   Illus: Viviana Barletta.
(Buenos Aires: Editorial Plus Ultra, 1978.   79 p.)
Gr. 4-7.

A seagull is upset because of the excess of civilization in the world and because of the lack of love among
various animal species.   She decides to go around the
world to help others recuperate their natural senses and
to learn to love each other.   Monotonously, the author
reminds the reader: "La Bondad, la Generosidad, la
Tolerancia, el Amor a los padres y a todos los seres
que se nos parecen y a los que no se nos parecen, ya
están inventados.   En realidad, están desde los comien-
zos de la Creación.   Pero a veces nos olividamos de
ello.   [Kindness, Generosity, Tolerance, Respect, Love
to our parents and all Beings who are like us and those
that are unlike us; all have been invented.   In reality,
they have been here from the beginnings of Creation.
But sometimes we forget.]"   p. 34.   The appealing animal illustrations are the only redeeming quality in this
otherwise dull sermon.

nr _____.   Historias de ositos.   Illus: Luis Pollini.
(Buenos Aires: Editorial Plus Ultra, 1979.   47 p.)
Gr. 1-3.

This book includes seven stories about little bears
which are dull, tedious reading.   Young children will
not find the long, rambling text appealing and older children will not be entertained by little bears that constantly
ask why or what for or who don't wish to do anything.
The author's moralistic admonitions further detract from
the enjoyment of these stories.   The following is the end-

ing of the story, "The Little Bear, Why?": "No sólo
que dijo la verdad, que es tan lindo, sino que él solo
dió la respuesta correcta.   Aprender a contestar uno
solito las preguntas pequeñas y sencillas, eso se llama
crecer. [Not only did he tell the truth, which is so nice,
but he alone gave the correct answer. To learn to answer oneself short and simple questions, that is called
growing up.]" p. 11.

nr _____. Morrongo, el gato sin botas y otros cuentos.
Illus: Kitty Lorefice de Passalia. (Buenos Aires: Editorial Guadalupe, 1978. 60 p.) Gr. 3-5.

   This includes four stories about Morrongo, the cat
without boots, which will not amuse young readers. Only
the first story was written with the intention of entertaining children: It tells about a very poor cat who got the
king to give every kitten in the kingdom a pair of shoes
even though he himself only selected a pair of sandals.
The other stories are much slower and, to make matters
worse, the endings are stilted moralistic messages to
young readers; for example: "Costó convencer a Gatobién que los pequeños--y grandes--triunfos en la vida no
se consiguen gracias a talismanes de la buena suerte,
sino a capacidad y talento.   Y que tampoco la capacidad
y talento se adquieren con un 'golpe de suerte,' sino después de mucho trabajo, estudio y entusiasmo. [It was
hard to convince Gatobién that the small--and large--
successes in life are not obtained thanks to good luck
charms but to skill and talent. And that skill and talent
are not acquired by a 'stroke of luck,' but after much
work, study, and enthusiasm.]" unnumbered page.
There are additional messages to young readers: avoid
boredom by hard work, help your fellow creatures, and
others.   A few black-and-white illustrations complement
the long text.

nr Carbalho, González. Jardín perdido.   (Buenos Aires:
Editorial Plus Ultra, 1979. 143 p.) Gr. 9-12.

   These brief thirty-three stories are intended as a
homage to its author upon his twentieth death anniversary.
They are sentimental reminiscences of the author's childhood in which he describes his thoughts and feelings about
childhood, that lost garden; Elsa, his little friend, who

caught a blue butterfly; Miss Clementina, his understanding and tolerant teacher; Pibe, his loyal and intelligent
dog; and other nostalgic reflections. Perhaps adults who
treasure the memory of González Carbalho will enjoy
these reminiscences; however, I am afraid that young
readers will not be interested in these autobiographical
memories of someone's childhood.

*   Cervantes Saavedra, Miguel de. Aventuras de Don Quijote para los niños. (Buenos Aires: Editodos, 1978.
61 p.) Gr. 8-12.

This is an excellent adaptation for young readers of
Cervantes' masterpiece. It includes Don Quijote's well-
known adventures in the order in which they appear in
the original version. The modern style and vocabulary
used in this simplified account make it a most enjoyable
and witty introduction to Spain's best loved novel, El
ingenioso Hidalgo Don Quijote de la Mancha.

nr   Cupit, Aarón, and Susana Gesumaría. Cuentos argentinos para jóvenes. (Buenos Aires: Editorial Plus Ultra,
1979. 127 p.) Gr. 8-10.

The authors wrote this collection of fourteen short
stories because they "believe that there is a need for a
different literature for adolescents ... without violence,
fear, terror or volatile mannerisms ... with truth, reality and true juvenile feelings. " This resulted in presumptuous stories which philosophize to young readers
about life, personal freedom, youth, nature, and other
"important" subjects. The stories lack interest and the
writing style is even worse. The following is an example of a dialogue between a young man and an adult:

"Si tuvieras que elegir entre vivir al pie de una
montaña o en la parte mas alta, ¿qué preferirías?
-- En lo más alto.
-- Sí ..., es muy lindo. Muchos tratan de su-
bir, algunos llegan. Tal vez la vida sea más feliz
en los valles, o en las laderas.

[If you had to choose between living at the foot of
a mountain or the highest part, which would you prefer?
-- At the highest part.

-- Yes ... it is very nice. Many try to go up;
some make it. Perhaps life is happier on the valleys or on the slopes.]" p. 65.

nr _____. Un televisor de largas orejas. (Buenos
Aires: Aique Grupo Editor, 1980. 67 p.) Gr. 5-8.

In this collection of five short stories the author ex-
presses his not so subtle moralistic messages to young
readers: "Un televisor de largas orejas" is about a boy
who describes his preference for a ball instead of a TV
set: "[P]refiero la pelota. Juego con ella y me hace
caso. La arrojo y vuelve, la dejo caer y sube, la tiro
al aire y viene a mis manos.... ¿Acaso puedo jugar
con la televisión? [I prefer the ball. I play with her
and she pays attention to me. I throw her, and she returns; I drop her, and she rises; I throw her to the
wind, and she comes to my hands.... By chance can I
play with the TV set?]" p. 5-6.
Other stories describe "adventures" in an empty lot,
the friendly attitudes of a "wild" monkey, the feelings of
a young boy about a new freeway, and the thoughts of a
boy who learned not to be afraid.
Fortunately, neither the moralistic text nor the unappealing illustrations will attract young readers to these
stories.

m Daireaux, Godofredo, and others. Cuentos de adolescentes.
(Buenos Aires: Editorial Kapelusz, 1978. 111 p.) Gr.
10-adult.

Most of the authors represented in this collection of
six short stories wrote in the early 1900's. Angel Mazzei selected the following stories because they describe
"the age of conflict and search for a life style that is
evident of adolescence": "El hombre del fogón" by Godofredo Daireaux, "La selva de los reptiles" by Joaquín V.
González, "Vidalita" by Mateo Booz, "La sombra del pastor"
by Pablo Rojas Paz, "El minuet" by Luisa Mercedes
Levinson, and "La muerte inventada" by María Angélica
Bosco.
Some adults may be interested in the thirty-five-page
critical essay and introduction written by Angel Mazzei
in which he discusses adolescence, literature, and Argentine authors. Sophisticated young adults will be interested
in the variety of themes that these brief stories relate.

m   Denevi, Marco. Robotobor. Illus: Antonio Berni.
      (Buenos Aires: Editorial Crea, 1980. 64 p.) Gr. 7-9.

      The Fernández family suddenly finds that a robot is
      living in their home: The children are delighted because
      they can play with him; Lily, the mother, is delighted
      because he can cook dinner; and Doctor Amormio, the
      father, is delighted because he can practice computerized
      medicine. So, when the robot breaks down, it affects
      the whole family, and they learn that "technology is im-
      portant, but not that much. "
      This story has an interesting plot; it is, however,
      too verbose and overdrawn. The illustrations add a much
      needed lightness to the lengthy descriptions.

m   Devetach, Laura. Picaflores de cola roja. Illus: Juan
      Marchesi. (Buenos Aires: Ediciones de la Flor, 1980.
      28 p.) Gr. 3-5.

      Children who attend a traditional school in Buenos
      Aires are easily distracted: Instead of paying attention
      to their teacher's spelling dictation, they start playing
      with each other and passing candy around. Suddenly all
      the class is looking at the amazing hummingbirds that
      flew inside the classroom. The only one who could not
      see them was the teacher. Finally the children taught
      the teacher how to see hummingbirds: through a little
      hole in a dry leaf. The witty illustrations add gaiety to
      this simple story about children in a school setting.

nr   Durán, Carlos Joaquín. Cuentos en celeste y blanco.
      Illus: Gustavo Bech. (Buenos Aires: Editorial Plus
      Ultra, 1980. 59 p.) Gr. 2-4.

      This is a collection of six uninspired stories: One
      tells about a "magic" family that decides to travel out-
      side of Buenos Aires every weekend; others are about a
      monkey who learned to say hello, a river that sings,
      seagulls that search for food, a penguin's birthday party,
      and a dove who earned her living as a baker. The long,
      tedious text and the lifeless illustrations will certainly
      not appeal to young readers.

*   _____. Viaje al planeta misterioso. (Buenos Aires:
      Aique Grupo Editor, 1980. 64 p.) Gr. 5-8.

This is a simply-told science fiction story which includes a "good" robot, an inventor, his wife and two
children, and a "bad" scientist. They live in the year
3125 in a city where there wasn't a single green tree or
plant left: "Todo había sido plastificado, pavimentado,
desinfectado, aprovechado, techado y cerrado. [Every-
thing had been plastified, paved, disinfected, used, covered with a roof, and closed.]" p. 11.
When the family goes on vacation to a mysterious
planet, they encounter serious danger as the bad scientist wishes to kill them by changing the robot's signals.
The contrast of life in a highly developed planet and in
a planet which was full of "natural life" is a bit exaggerated, but the excitement of the story certainly main-
tains the reader's interest. Unoriginal textbook-like illustrations of outer space complement the text.

nr   Escofet, Cristina. Cyrano de la colina. Illus: Juan
     Carlos López. (Buenos Aires: Editorial Plus Ultra,
     1981. 78 p.) Gr. 8-10.

     These eleven slow-moving fantasy stories about a
thirteen-year-old girl, Trenchy, and her cat, Cyrano,
will put young readers to sleep. According to the editor, young readers will discover in these stories the
poetry and wisdom that is evident in all people, animals,
and things. I am afraid that young readers will not find
any of this in a war between salt and pepper or in
Trenchy's and Cyrano's dull adventures at the beach or
in any of the other insipid stories.

nr   Falbo, Graciela. Papelito violeta. Illus: Luis Pollini.
     (Buenos Aires: Editorial Plus Ultra, 1979.   48 p.)
     Gr. 3-5.

     This is a collection of six abstruse stories with long
descriptions in which nothing seems to happen. They
tell of a violet-colored paper that nobody wanted, a pud-
dle that became a sea, a little spider that was always
bored, an invisible rabbit that finally found a home, a
new chimney in a garden, and the day that the sky was
blue. Three-tone, lifeless illustrations complement the
equally spiritless text.

m   Finch, María Rosa. El señor Viento Otto. Illus: Ayax

Barnes. (Buenos Aires: Centro Editor de América Latina, 1978. 24 p.) Gr. 2-4.

This is the story of what happened when Mr. Otto, the Wind, went on strike: Ita, the ant, could not find food; Lloronón, the willow, could not refresh itself; little pigeons could not learn to fly; wheat fields could not dance any more; and little girls' hair would not blow with the wind. Stylistic, modern illustrations gracefully complement the story; however, the narration is often too complex to be comprehended by young readers.

nr   Finchelman, María Rosa. Cuenticosas de chiquimundo. Illus: Martica. (Buenos Aires: Editorial Plus Ultra, 1980. 78 p.) Gr. 5-8.

Twelve tedious, melodramatic stories that tell about the tenderness of a little tree that felt the pain and joy of growing up; the sadness of a little car because his owners wanted to exchange him for a big, black car; a proud book that finally learned to love; and others. Neither the slow-moving stories nor the lifeless three-tone illustrations will appeal to readers of any age.

nr   _____, and others. Desde Córdoba les contamos. Illus: Liotta. (Buenos Aires: Editorial Plus Ultra, 1981. 175 p.) Gr. 4-6.

Nine authors from the province of Córdoba in Argentina wrote these eighteen slow-moving stories about a blue balloon, a catcher of clouds, a day that lost its night, an enchanted moon, a singing cat and other absurd themes. Perhaps if the authors would greatly simplify the text, young children might find these stories of interest. The illustrations are appropriate for young readers.

nr   Finkel, Berta. ¡Chumbale, Bob! Illus: Amalia Cernadas. (Buenos Aires: Editorial Plus Ultra, 1980. 95 p.) Gr. 5-6.

These thirty-two lethargic stories are difficult to read by young children because of long, tedious descriptions and impossible to enjoy by older children because

of uninspired plots and characters. The stories are
about a boy's apartment, an elevator, a dream, a piece
of paper, after school, bread crumbs, a broken jar, and
other prosaic subjects. Child-like two-tone illustrations
complement each story.

nr _____. Titeretín y Titeretón. Illus: Mariel Rodríguez. (Buenos Aires: Editorial Plus Ultra, 1981. 47
p.) Gr. 4-6.

Twenty-four saccharine poems and stories about animals, balloons, soap bubbles, and the sea that could not
possibly interest fourth to sixth graders because of their
overly sweet descriptions and themes. Young children
will not be able to read the long text. The three-tone
illustrations are also sweet and innocent.

m Freda, Rafael. Los cruzados. Illus: Blas Alfredo
Castagna. (Buenos Aires: Editodos, 1978. 62 p.)
Gr. 9-12.

This story is an adaptation of Torcuato Tasso's epic
poem, Jerusalem Delivered. Freda has maintained the
excitement of the original poem: Thus it includes the
extraordinary courage of Godofredo, Armida's incredible
beauty, and countless medieval battles in which the cru-
saders fought the Turks and others in their efforts to
free the sacred city. Unfortunately, the story includes
too many characters and complicated situations that are
not easily understood in this sixty-page version. Black-
and-white engravings of medieval warriors and princesses
are an attractive complement to the text.

* Garrido de Rodríguez, Neli, ed. Cuentos de amor para
chicos (de 8 a 13 años). (Buenos Aires: Ediciones
Orión, 1978. 174 p.) Gr. 8-12.

This is a collection of fifteen love stories about
princes and princesses, legendary characters, and
modern boys and girls by well-known authors, such as
Rubén Darío, Washington Irving, Alejandro Casona, O.
Henry, Victoria Ocampo, Carlos Rodríguez Pintos, Manuel Mujica Lainez, María Alicia Domínguez, Susana López de Gomara, Susana Gesumaría, Carlos Joaquín Durán,

and Liliana Aguilar.   The brevity of these well-written stories will appeal to romantic readers who wish to read about love as expressed by various authors throughout the ages.

nr _____. Espuma y negrito.   Illus: Lisandro Martínez. (Buenos Aires: Editorial Plus Ultra,   1978.   48 p.)   Gr. 3-4.

This is a collection of ten slow-moving stories that tell about two horses that fell in love, an owl that wouldn't sleep during the day, a playful bird, a frog that lost its shadow, a cat that owned a drugstore, and other ludicrous animal stories.   The long text makes them unappealing to young children and boring to older readers. The illustrator assumed that these stories were written for very young children.

nr Gesumaría, Susana.   La flauta mágica de tía sola.   Illus: Viviana Barletta.   (Buenos Aires: Editorial Plus Ultra, 1979.   80 p.)   Gr. 5-7.

According to the introduction of these six uninspired stories, they will awaken the "magic" that is within all of us.   Thus, these stories tell about the magic of a dog that gives birth, the magic of an old watchmaker, the magic of a lonely boy, the magic of Aunt Sola's magic flute, and the magic of a cat.   I am afraid that most readers will find nothing but boredom in these obtuse stories with sluggish illustrations.

* _____. El gato de los ojos dorados.   (Buenos Aires: Aique Grupo Editor, 1980.   63 p.)   Gr. 6-10.

Three of the five stories included in this book will have a special appeal to teenage girls: "Sietecuernos" tells of a brave girl who gets rid of a gang of obnoxious teenage boys by displaying her talents as a bullfighter; "Espejito, querido espejo" is about the concerns of a thirteen-year-old girl regarding her own future and her first love; and "Los ojos de Papá Noel" describes Christmas Eve celebrations through the eyes of a mature girl who wanted to protect her little brother from being disappointed with "Papá Noel's" gifts.   The other two stories

are too ambiguous for young readers. Unfortunately, all
of the illustrations are bad; they are uncreative as well
as lifeless.

nr _____, and Aarón Cupit. Cuentos de frontera para
jóvenes. (Buenos Aires: Editorial Losada, 1981. 147 p.)
Gr. 9-12.

These twelve languid stories lack interest and real
characters. They tell about Nicasio and his newly-found
vicuña (a South American wool-bearing quadruped, celebrated for its wool), Aniceto and his bicycle, Analía and
her sick mother, two freedom-loving lions from Durazno,
and others.

m Giménez Pastor, Marta. La brujita Trik. Illus: Luis
Pollini. (Buenos Aires: Editorial Plus Ultra, 1978.
47 p.) Gr. 3-5.

These are the amusing adventures of a little witch
and a little girl, Marcela. Unfortunately, Marcela is
supposed to be starting first grade, and her interests
are those of a first grade child--she is learning to read,
and the illustrations show her with a teddy bear. Young
children, however, will not be able to read the long descriptions on every page. On the other hand, older
children might enjoy the little witch's pranks at school,
in the bus, at home, at the TV studio, and at a party.
Simple, three-tone illustrations complement the text.

nr _____. Corazón de galleta. Illus: Martica. (Buenos
Aires: Editorial Plus Ultra, 1981. 47 p.) Gr. 3-5.

These eleven uninspired, slow-moving stories tell
about a bird's wedding; a little boat; a little cookie; a
scarecrow who went to the moon; a beautiful rooster; the
night of the fireflies; Maria's monkey; Raulito, the gymnast; a little pink ribbon; a sick mailbox; and a boy who
dreams about camels. The saccharine, three-tone illustrations are as uninviting as the text.

nr _____. Queridos animalitos. Illus: Martica. (Buenos Aires: Editorial Plus Ultra, 1981. 47 p.) Gr. 4-6.

The six poems about animals included in this book might appeal to young children, as they simply describe an elephant, a hippopotamus, a giraffe, a lion, a bird, and a pigeon. The ten stories, however, are dull and lifeless: They tell of a little insect who plays in a garden, a little dog that had a blue foot, a flower that walked, an otter's little house, a stupid fox, a red button, and others. The three-tone illustrations of sweet little animals are insulting to older children. Nobody will enjoy the long, tedious text.

m Goldberg, Mirta. Corchito va por el mundo. Illus: Renata Schussheim. (Buenos Aires: Ediciones Altazor, 1978. 18 p.) Gr. 1-3.

The best part of this book is the charming four-tone illustrations of Corchito, a black beetle, and Cantoche, a cricket. Corchito decides to see the world and Cantoche teaches him to look for food and to hide from children. The story is much too slow, and the text uses unnecessary repetition to describe an event. The following is the author's description of what happens when Corchito found a big stone:

"[E]ncontró una piedra en el camino y quiso empujarla para poder seguir....
¡Fuerza con una pata!
¡Fuerza con la otra!
Pero no. No y no.
El no sabía que iba a encontrar piedras
¡Y mucho menos que no las podría mover!
Y lloró Corchito. "

nr Gori, Gastón. Y además, era pecoso.... (Buenos Aires: Librería Nuevo Best-Seller, 1977. 123 p.) Gr. 8-10.

In this collection of twenty sentimental short stories the author recounts his childhood. He writes about the pets he loved, the girl he liked, the pranks he got into, his best friend, the punishments he received from his father, and his feelings about his mother. He frequently describes her in the following manner: "[L]a fresca ternura de la mujer que más he admirado, y cuya deliciosa ingenuidad y su amable manera, no marchitan los años,

porque ella sabe amar a todos los seres y las cosas
con su inocente alegría. " [(T)he fresh tenderness of the
woman that I have most admired, and whose delightful
ingenuity and kind manner the years do not fade away,
because she knows how to love all beings and things with
her innocent happiness.] p. 122.

Perhaps some adults might enjoy reading these emo-
tionally-written reminiscences, but young readers will
certainly be turned off by the strong moralistic intent
of these stories.

* Gorostiza, Carlos. El barquito viajero. Illus: Blanca
Medda. (Buenos Aires: Editorial Kapelusz, 1978.
14 p.) Gr. 1-3.

Amusing rhymes and attractive illustrations tell the
story of a little boat that goes out to sea. The pas-
sengers get ready to board, its crew makes all the preparations, and the people who stay behind wave good-bye.
There is also a captain who is in charge, and finally the
arrival to a new port.

* _____. Los días de fiesta. Illus: Blanca Medda.
(Buenos Aires: Editorial Kapelusz, 1978. 14 p.) Gr.
1-3.

Various holidays well known to Hispanic children are
depicted through attractive illustrations and simple
rhymes. It includes New Year's Eve, the Three Wise
Men, carnivals, national holidays, birthdays, Columbus
day, and Christmas.

* _____. ¡Todos al zoológico! Illus: Blanca Medda.
(Buenos Aires: Editorial Kapelusz, 1978. 14 p.) Gr.
1-3.

Simple and witty rhymes tell about a child's visit to
the zoo. It includes amusing descriptions and colorful
illustrations of an elephant, a camel, a monkey, a peacock, a lion, a giraffe, a polar bear, and a hippopotamus. The following is part of an amusing rhyme describing a peacock:

"El pavo real pasea

> muy apuesto y elegante,
> mientras la cola menea
> porque se siente importante. "

nr   Granata, María.   El ángel que perdió un ala y otros
cuentos.   Illus: Adriana Frattantoni.   (Buenos Aires:
Editorial Acme, 1979.   205 p.)   Gr. 4- 6.

This includes twenty monotonous stories that tell
about an angel who lost a wing, a hungry mirror, a boy
who played with his guardian angel, a magician's dog,
and other vacuous stories.   The following ending of the
story "Las siete imágenes" is an example of this author's
drab writing style: "La felicidad fue inmensa para todos.
Los pájaros lo festejaban con sus cantos más alegres.
Y los siete niños volvieron a su casa sabiendo que la
casa es el lugar más hermoso del mundo. [Happiness
was enormous for everybody.   The birds celebrated it
with their most joyful songs.   And the seven children returned to their home knowing that home is the most beautiful place in the world.]"   p. 289.
A few prosaic illustrations are interspersed throughout the 205 pages of text.

nr   _____ .   El gallo embrujado y otros cuentos.   (Buenos
Aires: Editorial Acme, 1978.   189 p.)   Gr. 5- 7.

This is a collection of twenty-two lethargic stories
that tell about a bewitched rooster, a tree that lost its
memory, a poor river, a strange leaf, a repentant volcano, and other incredible "fantasy" stories.   The author's overly sentimental writing style and the incredible
plots will certainly not appeal to young readers.   The
following is an example of the author's style: "[E]l
árbol sintió que al cabo de tanto sufrimiento y de tanta
esperanza, un corazón muy dulce se formaba en el interior de su tronco.   [(T)he tree felt that after so much
suffering and so much hope, a very sweet heart was form-
ing in the inside of its trunk.]"   p. 43.   And after several pages of describing the tree's feelings, it quickly re-
covered its memory.

nr   _____ .   La ciudad que levantó vuelo.   Illus: Julia
Diaz.   (Buenos Aires: Editorial Crea, 1980.   60 p.)
Gr. 4- 6.

This is a complex and uninspired story of a maker
of wings. He made thousands of wings which he gave
to every roof, tree, and tower of his city. Suddenly his
son, Bimbo, is taken away by thousands of birds. What
follows is Bimbo's senseless adventures in outer space:
Bimbo encounters a young sun, Bimbo sees a flying dog,
an elephant wishes to see if the universe has a floor,
the arrival of a new satellite, and Bimbo's happy return
to Earth. So what does Bimbo want to be when he
grows up?--"Fabricante de alas" (a maker of wings).

*   Guait, Camilo. Furia de oro en el Páramo. Illus:
Blas Alfredo Castagna. (Buenos Aires: Ediciones Toqui, 1977. 42 p.) Gr. 6-10.

The fast-moving text and striking black-and-white
illustrations tell the story of the gold rush era in the
southernmost part of Argentina in the 1880's. It relates
well-known episodes of an unusual war between Julio Pop-
per, a Rumanian gold prospector, and many adventurers
in search of gold. Young readers will experience the adventures, dangers, and excitement which prevailed in Argentina before the establishment of the large farming es-
tates.

nr   Gudiño Kieffer, Eduardo. Felipito el furibundo filibus-
tero. Illus: Hugo Teruggi. (Buenos Aires: Editorial
Crea, 1980. 62 p.) Gr. 6-8.

Pepablo stayed with his lovely grandmother one summer while his parents went to Europe. Even though
Grandma knitted, read, cooked, and watered her plants,
she was an unusual grandmother. Especially when she
and Pepablo decide to explore the bottom of the sea.
There they found a pirate, a mermaid, an octopus, and
other marine fantasies. The long, complicated text
seems endless, and there is a lack of interest in these
sluggish marine "adventures. " The only bright aspect
of this fantasy are the colorful illustrations.

nr   Gutiérrez, Josefina Estrella. El sapito no sé cuantos.
Illus: Luis Pollini. (Buenos Aires: Editorial Plus Ultra, 1979. 47 p.) Gr. 2-4.

These three saccharine animal stories lack interest, as nothing seems to happen. One tells of a very "good" toad that one day walked and walked without knowing where he was going: "Hay que seguir, sin detenerse, sin sentir el cansancio, hay que seguir hasta que el buen Dios disponga otra cosa. [One must continue without stopping, without feeling tired; one must continue until the good Lord orders otherwise.]" p. 5. When the toad decided to get married, he fell in love, looked at his bride-to-be, and then went in search of a rainbow with her. The second story tells about two squirrels that went on a long bicycle trip where they encountered many animals. The last story tells how a pine tree became a Christmas tree. The long descriptions, lack of action, and overly sentimental characters make these stories dull and monotonous reading. The three-tone illustrations are as uninspired as the text.

m   Kieffer, Cristina Gudino. La descomunal batalla de Don Quijote. Illus: Oscar Grillo. (Buenos Aires: Centro Editor de América Latina, 1977. 32 p.) Gr. 4-6.

In a modern, easy-to-understand text the author relates a few of the adventures from the famous Don Quijote. There are brief descriptions of Don Quijote, Sancho Panza, Rocinante, the battle against the sheep, an encounter with the "Caballero de los Espejos," and a defense of Dulcinea's beauty. Unfortunately, the illustrations are disfigured images of unappealing characters in bold colors. The wit and wisdom of Cervantes' classic are not present in this story.

nr   Kuyumdjian, Felisa. La niña y la mariposa. Illus: Ricardo Pasteur Longo. (Buenos Aires: Editorial Plus Ultra, 1981. 79 p.) Gr. 7-9.

The girl in this story represents all children or "all human beings who are learning about life," and the butterfly represents the soul: "that which will teach the girl to capture the deepest, most beautiful, and generous part of life." So, "each episode signifies the achievement of spiritual maturity--the growth in values that go beyond material values." Neither the stale, three-tone illustrations nor the affected text make this story entertaining reading.

nr   Lacau, María Hortensia.   Con algo de magia.   (Buenos
     Aires: Editorial Plus Ultra, 1979.   111 p.)   Gr. 9-12.

       The author wrote this collection of nine love stories
     to convey to young readers her thoughts about the "magic
     of love." Therefore, all her stories emphasize love to
     life and its many riches, the reconquest of love, love to
     others, the triumph of life and love, the beginning of a
     new love, the magic of adolescent love, and, lastly, the
     magic of love in marriage.
       The melodramatic writing style and the author's ob-
     session with the "magic of love" result in a most ex-
     travagant combination. The following, for example, is
     the author's description of when a man first feels the
     magic of love: "Así es la vida.... Siempre hay tiempo
     para volver a encontrarse, para aprender. De pronto,
     llega un ser distinto, un ser con una llamita de humani-
     dad ... un ser absurdo, quizás, pero con algo de magia,
     y se produce un cambio que no se sabe bién qué es.
     [Such is life.... There is always time to find yourself
     again, to learn. Suddenly, a different being arrives, a
     being with a little flicker of humanity ... an absurd
     being, perhaps, but with some magic, and a change is
     produced that one doesn't know really what it is.]" p. 21.

nr   López de Gomara, Susana.   Niña Lucía.   (Buenos Aires:
     Editorial Plus Ultra, 1980.   79 p.)   Gr. 9-12.

       Melodramatically, the author reminisces about her
     childhood and teenage years: She introduces herself as
     an ugly, small girl, who wore glasses, who had no
     charms, and who was extremely shy. She explains that
     life is a continuation, that one is not a product of chance.
     Thus, she relates the influences that her parents, grand-
     parents, aunts, uncles, brothers, sisters, and other peo-
     ple exerted in her and produced the "suffering child that
     I was and the adult that I believe to be." She remem-
     bers how she enjoyed her mother's stories, her periods
     of sickness, her first communion, and other important
     times of her life.
       There is nothing here that will interest young read-
     ers.

nr   _____. Pajarito canta cuentos.   Illus: Chacha.   (Bue-
     nos Aires: Editorial Plus Ultra, 1978.   47 p.)   Gr. 2-4.

Tedious collection of poems and stories about singing birds, a wise turtle, a brave cat, a fat toad, a little mouse, and other things that should interest young children. However, the long descriptions, complex situations and unappealing characters will certainly not attract young children. The following is an example of this author's writing style: "¡Qué lindas, las flores del Jardín del Amanecer! Parecían venidas del cielo, esas rosas perfumadas, esas anémonas de ensueño, esos blancos alhelíes. [How beautiful, the flowers of the Garden of Sunrise! They appeared as if they came from the sky, those perfumed roses, those imaginative anemones, those white violets.]" p. 11. And after several sentences of the same, she continues to tell a slow-moving story about a little bird.

Writing such as this is boring to all readers--young or otherwise.

nr   Luján Campos, María Luisa de. Carozo hermoso. Illus: Roberto Broullon. (Buenos Aires: Editorial Plus Ultra, 1978. 47 p.) Gr. 3-4.

Nine saccharine stories with long tedious descriptions that tell about a beautiful teddy bear; a forgetful ant; a weeping frog; Anastasio, the elephant who polished shoes; a cricket who played the violin; and others. The endless text and moralistic admonitions are not conducive to enjoyable reading or listening. For example, the following is the ending of one of these stories: "[M]ientras empieza a darse cuenta de que, muchas veces, es necesario que las cosas salgan mal la primera vez para que luego sean realmente buenas. [(M)eanwhile, he begins to realize that many times it is necessary for things to turn up badly the first time, so that later they will really be good.]" p. 23.

nr   _____. Lauchín Bigotes. Illus: Diana Akselman. (Buenos Aires: Editorial Plus Ultra, 1981. 47 p.) Gr. 3-5.

These are twenty-three tedious stories and poems about Lauchín Bigotes, a mouse. Lauchín Bigotes likes to eat candy, play with butterflies, be friendly with stars, ride a flying pony, go to the moon, and say good-bye.

Children will find these stories and poems uninteresting, lengthy, and dull.

nr _____. El Pecoso. (Buenos Aires: Editorial Guadalupe, 1978. 175 p.) Gr. 9-12.

A young man from Argentina relates his sad life
which is full of misery and deprivation. The author
monotonously intermixes moralistic admonitions with
vague allusions to the value of life. For example, after
a depressing incident in which the main character (the
reader never knows his name) and his friend, Pecoso,
save a dog's life, he thinks: "Y entonces, sentí que era
una cosa muy seria hacerse hombre y empezar a luchar
por lo bueno y por lo justo. [And then, I felt that it
was a very serious thing to become a man and to fight
for what is good and for what is fair.]" p. 55. There
are a few chapters that tell about the main character's
grandfather, who was old and needy. Yet the author
only conveys a lethargic description of a man whose life
was "silently coming to an end. " Young readers will
certainly not be interested in a novel whose characters
are constantly looking for goodness in life and which
tries very hard to mix tenderness with a vague reality.

nr Marcuse, Aida. Un caballo a motor. Illus: Luis Pollini. (Buenos Aires: Editorial Plus Ultra, 1981. 48 p.)
Gr. 3-5.

This is a collection of seventeen abstract stories
and poems about a traveling leaf, wooden horses, a nest
for rent, sunset on the farm, and other listless topics.
The complicated vocabulary and difficult sentence construction further detract from their appeal to younger
readers.

nr Maritano, Alma. Un globo de luz anda suelto. Illus:
Amalia Cernadas. (Buenos Aires: Editorial Plus Ultra,
1978. 111 p.) Gr. 4-6.

Nicanor, a young boy from a small town in Argentina, tells about his magic world where he plays with
crystal balloons, little Indians, a ray of sunshine, a
flying wheel-barrow, and wooden horses. The second
part shows him adapting to life in the city and finding
out that there are also many fun things to do there. The
adventures described in this book would be of interest to
younger children if they were written in a simple, un-

sophisticated language that they could read and enjoy.
Unfortunately, the long descriptions and pages and pages
of text make this impossible.   The illustrations are much
simpler and will appeal to younger children.

*   Martín, Susana.   Mi primer amor.   (Buenos Aires: Editorial Plus Ultra, 1980.   95 p.)   Gr. 8-12.

Daniel is a sixteen-year-old boy from Buenos Aires.
His parents are Italian immigrants who find it very difficult to succeed in Argentina.   Daniel describes his
strong feelings towards Herminia, a neighbor and wonderful girl.   He also tells about life in his neighborhood,
his school, and his friends.   This novel has a slow start,
but it gains momentum towards the middle, when Daniel's
closest friend moves away from their neighborhood, and,
especially, when Daniel's father leaves home without
telling his mother where he is going.   Daniel's feelings
of insecurity as well as the economic difficulties he and
his mother experience after the father's departure are
very touchingly described.   Herminia, who remains constantly in the background, finally admits that she is fond
of Daniel.   And Daniel's anger and mixed feelings upon
his father's return several years later are genuine and
moving.

nr   .   Paula y la alfombra de piedra.   Illus: Liotta.
(Buenos Aires: Editorial Plus Ultra, 1980.   79 p.)   Gr.
5-8.

Paula, a kind and generous rabbit, is always anxious
to help others; consequently, in these eleven overly sentimental stories, we find Paula helping a little cat who
wishes to become a hunter, a glowworm who lost its
light, a robot and a witch who decide to work together,
a modern bee who learns that nature is wise and we
shouldn't attempt to change its customs, an old bear who
finally accepts the assistance of a younger helper, and a
dog who wishes to become a television star.   In the last
story all of Paula's friends send her gifts in appreciation
for her many kindnesses.   She thanks them for "showing
her that she is not alone" and because "they have not for-
gotten her."   Incredibly, children are again reminded to
help others.
Monotonous stories with saccharine illustrations that

will bore young readers with their obvious attempts to
indoctrinate.

m   . Yo quiero ser campeón. (Buenos Aires:
Editorial Plus Ultra, 1981. 93 p.) Gr. 9-12.

   Marcos, a young orphan boy, is paralyzed from the
waist down. He has lived in a hospital since he was
two months old with other boys who also couldn't walk.
The sadness and emptiness of their lives are briefly explained as well as their hopes and fears. Suddenly there
appears a marvelous young man--a nurse--who infuses
all of the boys with trust and a desire to exercise. Inexplicably, Marcos starts walking, leaves the hospital,
goes to live in Buenos Aires, experiences great luck as
well as tremendous deprivation, and assists his marvelous
friend in overcoming his own depression.
   Unfortunately, the author was too intent in teaching
young people that in life one must constantly persevere,
that nothing is easy, and that young people must work or
study. This novel has a lot of quick action, but it lacks
real characters--they all seem to symbolize desirable or
undesirable human traits with strong moralistic purposes.

nr Martínez, Paulina, and others. El patito Nicolás. Illus:
Luis Pollini. (Buenos Aires: Editorial Plus Ultra,
1981. 47 p.) Gr. 4-6.

   This is an insipid collection of seven stories that
tell about little ducks that learned how to swim, a little
boy who played with soap bubbles, a red wallet, a black
cat, a chick, an imaginary man, and a sparrow. The
long descriptions and lack of action in these stories will
certainly not appeal to children; the childish illustrations
further detract from them.

nr Marval, Carlota. Los Quitilipis. (Buenos Aires: Editorial Plus Ultra, 1978. 190 p.) Gr. 9-12.

   Quitilipi is the name of a town in the northern part
of Argentina, which is the setting for the first part of
this slow-moving novel. Perhaps because the author
tried to follow the norms suggested by the Ministry of
Culture and Education as to "adequate values" for young

adult readers in her description of characters and setting, the result is a tedious description of life in rural Argentina, the romance of a young couple in which Jacinto "must respect" Marisa, and the pain and suffering of Jacinto's grandmother, who is hospitalized and depends on Jacinto for her meager income.

m   Mereb, Juan.   Tubito y la pandilla cordobesa.   (Buenos Aires: Editorial Plus Ultra, 1980.   159 p.).   Gr. 8-10.

A successful doctor in his sixties relates his experiences as a child and teenager in his native city of Córdoba (Argentina) in the 1920's.   In thirty-two brief chapters he reminisces about his friends, summer holidays, trips to the movies, stealing fruit on the road to San Antonio, and other special occasions.   The natural and easy going style of this author is a pleasant exposure to the life of young people in Argentina sixty years ago.

nr   Moreno, Juan Carlos.   Cuentos de navidad y año nuevo. (Buenos Aires: Editorial Plus Ultra, 1978.   95 p.) Gr. 8-10.

The author wrote this collection of eight moralistic short stories for the purpose of entertaining young readers or for making them "cry a little for some of the characters in these stories. "   Most of the stories profess thanks to God for helping very poor children receive a few toys at Christmas, others tell about children who suffer hunger in various countries, and others tell about proud parents of very good and obedient children.   The author insists on boring readers with his constant messages.
    The following is an example of this author's writing style.   It is the end of a story in which a young man decides to marry a fat girl after all: "Y la verdad es ésta: que la mujer no vale por su apariencia, por su gordura o por su flacura, sino por su gracia, su habilidad y la belleza de su alma.   Al final, todas las mujeres, hasta las más hermosas, se marchitan.   [And the truth is this: that a woman's worth is not in her appearance, neither in her fatness nor slimness, but in her grace, in the ability and beauty of her soul.   At the end, all women, even the most beautiful, wither.]"   p. 34.   And so

on and on the author continues exalting "true beauty. "
Melodramatic illustrations of angelic children and suffering mothers make this book a sure bore.

nr   Murillo, José. Cuentos para mis hijos. Illus: Nidia
     Brandolin and others. (Buenos Aires: Bureau de Pro-
     motion, 1979. 157 p.) Gr. 5-8.

          The author's purpose in writing these ten stories is
     "to enrich the intelligence and sensitivity of young read-
     ers through lessons of life, love, and solidarity. " Hence,
     the stories tell about a dog that risks its life to save a
     child, and how other forest animals protect humanity
     through acts of genuine courage. The obvious intent of
     these stories makes them dull and tedious reading.

nr   _____ . Silvestre y el hurón. (Buenos Aires: Edi-
     ciones Lihuel, 1979. 143 p.) Gr. 6-8.

          Silvestre, a young, lonely boy who lives on a farm
     in Argentina, is delighted when he finds a newly-born
     ferret. They develop a close friendship in which the fer-
     ret follows Silvestre everywhere he goes. The ferret is
     loved by all the children in school. Silvestre's mother
     and teachers insist on teaching him about the importance
     of living things and respecting even the littlest and most
     insignificant because: "El equilibrio de la naturaleza
     está basado in ello.... El hombre ... tiene la respon-
     sabilidad de velar porque ese equilibrio no se altere.
     [Nature's equilibrium is based on it.... Man ... has
     the responsibility to watch carefully so that that equilibri-
     um does not alter.]" p. 130-131. Hence, Silvestre re-
     turns the ferret to the mountain.
          Slow-moving story about children, animals, and life.

nr   Neira, Luis. Un amigo de papel. Illus: Broullon.
     (Buenos Aires: Editorial Plus Ultra, 1980. 47 p.)
     Gr. 4-6.

          These eight odd fantasy stories tell about two chil-
     dren who became friendly with a paper doll; a little girl
     who saved her toys and dog from a flood; Peter, a cloud,
     and a cat and their many conversations; Peter's little
     turtle who searched for a home during her long nap; and

others.   These sluggish stories are as uninteresting as
the insipid illustrations.

m   Pardo Belgrano, María Ruth.   Dimensiones del amor.
     (Buenos Aires: Editorial Plus Ultra, 1979.   167 p.)
     Gr. 9-12.

     Various aspects of love are expressed in this collec-
     tion of stories, poems, and essays written by Hispanic
     authors from the sixteenth century until modern times.
     It includes the search for love, love and jealousy, com-
     mitment, friendship, love to country, love and death, and
     divine love.   Some of the authors represented are Rubén
     Darío, Juan Ramón Jiménez, Lope de Vega, Federico
     García Lorca, Gabriela Mistral, Fray Luis de León,
     Jorge Luis Borges, Miguel Buñuel, and others.

nr   Pelayo, Felix.   Historias para adolescentes.   (Buenos
     Aires: Ediciones Corregidor, 1980.   135 p.)   Gr. 7-10.

     This includes five listless stories about a dog and a
     wasp, five boys in search of adventures, an ice cream
     seller, a boy's holidays, and a boat, all of which lack
     real characters as well as believable plots.   The elabo-
     rate writing style further detracts from the appeal of
     these stories; for example: "Se los han ganado por su
     honradez tan espontáneamente demostrada y por la bondad
     de sus corazones.   [They have earned it for their hon-
     esty so spontaneously demonstrated and for the kindness
     in their hearts.]"   p. 48.

nr   Poletti, Syria.   Marionetas de asserín.   Illus: Clara
     Urquijo.   (Buenos Aires: Editorial Crea, 1980.   62 p.)
     Gr. 6-8.

     Ninín, a poor, happy girl, is anxious to have a pup-
     pet theater.   Miraculously her guardian angel gets her
     the puppets, and Ninín gives a performance for all the
     children and adults in her town.   The story ends by
     Ninín thinking that the puppets were really not puppets--
     they were characters "that one invents when one listens
     and looks within oneself; when one imagines a more beau-
     tiful world. "   This is a slow-moving story with tedious
     descriptions and complicated vocabulary.   The saccharine

illustrations of angelic children cannot do much to im-
prove it.

nr   . El misterio de las valijas verdes.   Illus:
Gusi. (Buenos Aires: Editorial Plus Ultra, 1978.
111 p.)   Gr. 7-9.

This absurd mystery story tells how a family of puppet players gets involved in a huge bank robbery.   Unbelievably, this family--a grandfather, mother, and four
children--were "so happy" that they "hadn't even noticed
how poor they were. "   They were invited to perform out-
side of Buenos Aires when some criminal-types exchanged
their bags at the railroad station.   Thus they were involved in a senseless "let's-find-our-bags story. "   Pe-
lusa, a "good" thief, was enchanted by the grace of the
blue fairy, by Snow White, and by the play that the puppet players were going to perform.   And here the author
inserts a three-page moral.   The following is the last
paragraph: "La música, el canto, la danza, la poesía
eran su clave.   Eran el misterio que daba a los ter-
restres la seguridad en un destino de amor.   Tal vez
era su manera de acercarse a Dios, como la plegaria,
la que nace de adentro.   Eso era tan único y tan valido
que bastaba para salvar la tierra de toda destrucción.
[Music, song, dance, poetry--those were his key.   They
were the mystery that gave people from the earth the
security of a destiny of love.   Perhaps it was their way
of approaching God, as a prayer that is born from within.
That was so unique and so valid that it was enough to
save the earth from all destruction.]"   p. 57.   Neither
the tedious moralizing nor the silly mystery will appeal
to readers of any age.

nr   Ramb, Ana María.   Un zapato con ceniza y lluvia.   (Buenos Aires: Editorial Plus Ultra, 1981.   141 p.)   Gr.
9-12.

This is a spiritless collection of ten short stories
that supposedly describe to young readers "real emotions,
conflicts, dreams, contradictions, and realities. "   The
stories, however, abound in numb plots and unreal characters.   For example, in "Candombe de José" a group
of teenagers are in search of "adventure and mystery" in
an old abandoned house, and in "En la tibieza" a girl discovers "love. "

nr   Ricci, Ferdinando. Gorjito el niño pájaro. (Buenos
     Aires: Editorial Plus Ultra, 1978.   126 p.) Gr. 6-8.

     Gorjito, a boy, was born the size of a worm and
later was adopted by sparrows. Long descriptions and
absurd situations tell about Gorjito's life among sparrows,
Indians, on an island of birds, and Gorjito, the liberator
of birds. Young readers will certainly not enjoy the
senseless plot nor the pedantic writing style. The following is a brief description of how Gorjito encourages other
birds not to be afraid of freedom: "--¡Vamos--les decía
--no sean cobardes! Es hora de que aprendan a amar
la libertad. Por culpa de algunos, la pierden muchos....
['Come on,' he told them, 'don't be cowards! It is time
that you learn to love liberty. It is the fault of some
that many lose it....']" p. 111.

nr   _____. Gorjito entre los hombres. (Buenos Aires:
     Editorial Plus Ultra, 1978.   70 p.) Gr. 8-12.

     Gorjito, a little man that flies and talks like a bird,
is the adopted son of sparrows. In this stale story, he
describes to man "the suffering of these beautiful creatures as they see themselves in captivity. " So, Gorjito
takes a trip around the world, hoping that he can convince
presidents, kings, and queens to prohibit the persecution
of birds and to allow them to be free. Finally he succeeds, and the birds' fear and terror disappear. The
following is the story's trite ending: "Pero el rey de
las aves comprendió que la lucha por la libertad no
terminaría jamás. [But the king of the birds realized
that the fight for liberty will never end.]" p. 67.
     Even birds will be bored with this story.

nr   Ricotti, Carmela. Jujuy naranja. (Buenos Aires: Edi-
     torial Plus Ultra, 1981.   79 p.) Gr. 6-10.

     This is a collection of brief short stories and poems
which tell about the author's "mysterious and magical
world. " In the introduction she asks the reader if he/
she is prepared for the "ingenuousness and amazement"
which follows as she writes about birds, a river, and
some personal remembrances, including a story about a
birth of a donkey. Some poems and stories tell about an
old box, sunrises, roads, and men: "Y el hombre amó,

y amó y amó.... [And the man loved, and loved and
loved....]" p. 72. Perhaps the author enjoyed writing
about her native province in Argentina; however, I don't
believe this collection will entertain or appeal to young
readers.

nr Roa Bastos, Augusto. Los juegos 1: "Carolina y Gas-
    par. " (Buenos Aires: Ediciones de la Flor, 1979.
    [30 p.]) Gr. 2-4.

    Carolina and Gaspar were very poor students in
school. Therefore, their parents had them study every
afternoon with a tutor. They disliked their tutor, as
she insisted on teaching them about dead insects, when
they only wanted to play and dream. Carolina's and
Gaspar's games and fantasies are tediously described in
this story: They play with mirrors and Coke bottles;
they play language games; and they invent a strange and
difficult game: the "rachacha-tum-tum-volarum-volarum. "
Thus, the children convinced their parents that "it is
beautiful to play games. " Appropriately senseless illustrations complement the senseless text.

m   Rubio, Gladys M. de. Pichi Nahuel: pequeño tigre ma-
    puche. Illus: Chacha. (Buenos Aires: Editorial Plus
    Ultra, 1981. 47 p.) Gr. 5-7.

    Pichi Nahuel, a little Indian from Argentina, is brave
and energetic. He wanted to become a great warrior like
his father, Vuta Nahuel, so he devoted much time to
learn how to shoot a bow and arrow. When his grandfather got sick, Pichi Nahuel rode long distances to get
him the birds' eggs he needed. He played with his
friends, and he helped his mother build a new house.
    Pichi Nahuel is a charming boy who will certainly
appeal to young readers. It is unfortunate, though, that
there is no continuity to his adventures. Rather, this
book includes a few isolated stories, poems, and riddles--
some about Pichi Nahuel and others about the moon, fish,
a little horse, and other animals.

nr Saraví, Luis Patricio. Los eternos pibes. (Buenos
    Aires: Editorial Plus Ultra, 1981. 79 p.) Gr. 9-12.

Five of the six narrations collected in this volume
are uninteresting: They tell of indigenous horses, civi-
lized dogs, and local heroes. The affected writing style
of this author certainly detracts from their appeal. The
only interesting essay is the last one, "Un hombre y una
mujer" (One man and one woman), which tells about the
courting and mating habits of the Indians of the pampas.

nr Seija, Simone. Le cuento a mi osito. Illus: Luis Ma-
tías Uraga. (Buenos Aires: Goyanarte Editor, 1978.
54 p.) Gr. 4-6.

These eight melodramatic, moralistic stories were
supposedly written by a ten-year-old girl and illustrated
by a nine-year-old boy. They tell of a sad little house
who did not want anybody living in it; a naughty little
horse; Juanito, the zoo guardian; a family of rabbits;
Mother Hen and her brave little chicks; a capricious doll;
and a loving teddy-bear.
Adults might be impressed by these stories written
by a child; children, however, will be bored by their
sluggishness and constant moralizing. The illustrations
are obviously done by a creative child.

nr Solves, Hebe. Pedacitos de tiempo. Illus: Hebe Solves.
(Buenos Aires: Editorial Plus Ultra, 1981. 77 p.) Gr.
5-8.

This is a lethargic collection of twenty-eight stories
and poems about animals, grandmothers, an apple, a
street, a ball, and others which are supposed to contain
the message that "there is magic everywhere, if one
knows how to look and listen to the silent language of
things and the voices of plants, animals, and places. "
The result are slow-moving stories and poems which lack
action and interest. They are accompanied by stale,
three-tone illustrations.

*   Sorrentino, Fernando. Cuentos del mentiroso. Illus:
Viviana Barletta. (Buenos Aires: Editorial Plus Ultra,
1978. 95 p.) Gr. 8-12.

These are two amusing stories about the amazing
liar Lelio García: The first one narrates Lelio's spec-

tacular adventures in Arizona, where he learns about the
existence of Billy the Kid. There he was captured by
the "Milwaukee" Indians as he tried to save Becky, a
beautiful girl. Upon the ungratefulness of Becky's father,
Lelio decides to leave Arizona and go to China. The
second story described Lelio's undertakings in China during the government of Aladdin and the Thousand and One
Nights. He tells how he was admired in the court of
the Sultan, Aladdin; how he became emperor of China;
and how, after ruling the destinies of China for some
time, he decided to return to Buenos Aires.

The light-hearted and witty text as well as the laugh-
able incidents and characters make these stories fun and
diverting. The few jovial, three-tone illustrations are in
tune with the stories.

m   Terrera, Alejandro. La ranita que creció al revés y
     otros cuentos. (Buenos Aires: Editorial Plus Ultra,
     1979. 79 p.) Gr. 3-5.

     Four animal stories that might appeal to some chil-
dren, although they deal with topics that only very young
children will find amusing: a little frog that changed
colors; a heroic ant that saved an anthill from starving;
and a tiny "sheriff" that frightened a witch, a dragon,
ghosts, and giants. Small, colorful animal illustrations
add a light touch to the text.

nr   Tibaudin, Aldo. Mosquita. Illus: by children. (Buenos
     Aires: Ediciones Hombre y Camino, 1980. 63 p.) Gr.
     4-6.

     Neither the poor presentation of this publication--
cheap paper, mimeographed copy, black-and-white children's illustrations--nor the long, lifeless stories will
appeal to readers. They tell of Mosquita, a kind, courageous dog; noisy birds; why foxes now have an unpleasant
odor; and why trains and stars get along.

nr   Vega, Adriana. Pericón anda en las uvas. (Buenos
     Aires: Editorial Plus Ultra, 1979. 159 p.) Gr. 7-9.

     This slow-moving story describes the childhood of
Nina and Pepita in a small town in Argentina. It tells

about their experiences in school with a very kind teacher,
their fears of ghosts, various nature trips that they took
with their classmates, and a fire in a nearby lumber mill
which makes Nina cry. She explains why: "'No lloro
por lo que se pierde. Me emociona ver como ayudan
las personas.' La sensibilidad de Nina percibe la noble
acción de ese pueblo. Todos parecen hormiquitas labori-
osas en común tarea. Como si algo les perteneciera
también. Es gente que ama a su trabajo. ['I don't cry
for what is lost. I am thrilled to see how people help.'
The sensitivity of Nina perceives the noble actions of
these people. Everybody looks like industrious ants shar-
ing a job. Like if it belonged to them, too. They are
people that love their work.]" p. 97.

Adolescents will be surely bored by these saccharine
stories of an ecstatic childhood.

nr Villafañe, Javier. <u>Cuentos con pájaros.</u> (Buenos Aires:
Hachette, 1978. 125 p.) Gr. 4-6.

These ten monotonous stories pretend to describe
the lifestyle and special characteristics of different types
of birds. As fiction they are unbelievable stories: They
tell incredible incidents about birds in strange situations,
such as why the bird known in Argentina as the "brasita
de fuego," "had the glory of having rested in the hands
of God," and why owls cannot talk any more and must
hide during daytime. Inert, two-tone illustrations complement the uninspired text.

*   Walsh, María Elena. <u>Chaucha y Palito.</u> Illus: Vilar.
(Buenos Aires: Editorial Sudamericana, 1977. 169 p.)
Gr. 5-9.

The author's marvelous, witty, alluring style will delight readers in this collection of six science fiction
stories about a castle in the sky; Felipito, who was anxious to become a "gaucho"; a group of fifth graders who
saved a colony of octopi by giving them all their hair; a
huge iguana that gained the affection of a poor family;
and the amazing love story between Aniceta and a colonel.
However, the best part of this book is the author's autobiography which comprises the last eighteen pages. In
it, María Elena Walsh relates her years as a child and
adolescent in Buenos Aires, her travels to New York and

Europe, and important incidents which affected her professional and personal development. Amusing illustrations complement the text.

LEGENDS

m Allassia, María Guadalupe. Paí-Luchí: cuentos del
   litoral. (Buenos Aires: Editorial Plus Ultra, 1980.
   85 p.) Gr. 9-12.

   These nineteen brief traditional stories and legends
   relate the adventures of Paí-Luchí, a well-known character of the Santa Fe Guaraní region of Argentina. He is
   witty, ingenious, and cunning and gets involved in strange
   feats, especially if it means taking adventage of various
   situations for his own benefit. It includes stories about
   Paí-Luchí overcoming ferocious tigers and Paí-Luchí
   barely escaping angry farmers. Some of the stories are
   fast-moving and entertaining; others are sluggish and uninteresting.

m Bendersky, Manuel, and others. Vamos a leer, Río
   Negro. (Buenos Aires: Editorial Plus Ultra, 1979.
   92 p.) Gr. 4-6.

   The purpose of this collection of seven stories was
   to recreate for children popular legends and beliefs of
   the Province of Río Negro in Argentina. Unfortunately,
   the authors seemed to be unduly concerned about the educational purposes of their stories, hence the stories lack
   the spontaneous joy of the original legends. There are
   stories about a male witch, a sacred tree, a wicked
   skunk, a singing snail, and a lucky tree. The following
   is an example of one of the moralistic endings: "En
   esta casa no entrará nunca la desgracia, porque crece
   el maitén y porque los niños saben buscar la buena suerte
   trabajando. [Adversity will never enter in this house,
   because the lucky tree grows and because children know
   that they must search for good luck by working.]" p. 87.
   A few uninspired three-tone illustrations complement
   the stories.

* Garrido de Rodríguez, Neli. Leyendas argentinas. Illus:
   José Miguel Heredia. (Buenos Aires: Editorial Plus Ultra, 1981. 111 p.) Gr. 6-10.

Delightful collection of nineteen pre-Columbian legends from South America that are simply written. They tell of how violence between two tribes was turned into friendship thanks to Onagait's beautiful messenger, the birth of delicate flowers, how dancing was invented, the punishment of the treacherous "Curupí," the love between a graceful princess and a valiant warrior, a little girl who made rain, and other entertaining legends.

The fast-pace and alluring characters make these legends a charming introduction to the people and natural resources of South America. The only unappealing part of this book are the awkward two-tone illustrations.

* Guait, Camilo. La fantástica historia de Jimmy Button. Illus: Blas Alfredo Castagna. (Buenos Aires: Ediciones Toqui, 1977. 46 p.) Gr. 5-9.

This is the fantastic story of three Yámana Indian boys and one girl who were left on board a British vessel in 1826. One of them died shortly afterwards. The others were taken to England, dressed like Europeans, and presented to the King and Queen of England. Although some people treated them as savages, the King and Queen were impressed by their politeness and gave Fueguia, the girl, a wedding trousseau. A few years later they returned to Argentina. One of the boys, York Minster, and Fueguia fell in love and got married; the other, Jimmy Button, became the controversial leader of the Yámana Indians. Some believed he killed many of his former English friends; others believed he simply remained confused as to which was a better life--the English or his tribe.

This is a well-told legend, with bold black-and-white illustrations, which will impress readers with its depiction of life in the southernmost tip of Argentina in the early 1800's.

* Martínez, Paulina, and others. Leyendas argentinas. Illus: Csecs. (Buenos Aires: Editorial Sigmar, 1977. 60 p.) Gr. 7-12.

This is a delightful collection of thirty-seven folk tales and legends from many Argentine provinces. The authors are to be commended for selecting a marvelous variety of tales and for preserving their authenticity.

At the end of each tale, the authors have explained the
meaning of words that refer specifically to some regions
of Argentina or to pre-Columbian times. It includes animal tales as well as tales from Patagonia, Mendoza,
Córdoba, and many other provinces that recount ancient
beliefs and customs. The simple, readable writing style
of these tales make them a most enjoyable overview of
Argentina. Colorful illustrations complement each tale.

m   Marval, Carlota. El país de los cielos mojados. (Buenos Aires: Editorial Plus Ultra, 1980.   125 p.)   Gr.
9-12.

Twelve legends from Argentina that tell about princes
and princesses, magic trees, kind ghosts amazing animals, and enchanting women. The wide variety of themes
and historical epochs represented in these legends might
appeal to some readers. Not all of the legends included
in this collection are interesting to read; the following,
however, have maintained their originality and fast-pace:
"El sombrerudo, " "La flor de Lirolay, " and "La mala
sombra. "

m   Milano, Patricio. Tandil en la leyenda ... (y en la historia). Illus: Miguel A. Desilio and Patricio Milano.
(Tandil: Impresora Vitullo, 1978.   67 p.) Gr. 8-12.

This is a collection of seven legends and stories
from Tandil, a town approximately 120 miles south of
Buenos Aires, which relates strange occurrences, the
courage of beautiful women, and the settling of the
"pampa" (the Argentine plains). Unfortunately, the format and illustrations do not add much to these stories:
the few black-and-white illustrations are uninspired de-
signs, and the type seems to be crowded in. The legends and stories, however, will incite young readers to
find out more about the natural scenic wonders which are
described in these stories.

*   Murillo, José. Leyendas para todos. (Buenos Aires:
Editorial Guadalupe, 1978.   143 p.) Gr. 9-adult.

This is a collection of eight legends from South America that have maintained their originality and fascination.

They tell about the enchanted house of Humahuaca, which
has maintained the secret of an unrequited love; the magic of "quenas" (small flutes made out of reed) in com-
bating loneliness; an evil ghost who lives in the bottom
of wells; fairies who protect shepherds; how death was
defeated in Atamisqui; the treasure that is hidden forever
in the "Laguna de Leandro"; a monster that unexpectedly
attacks men on lonely roads; and how a whole town was
punished because of its immorality.

The fast-pace of these legends make them engrossing
as well as enjoyable reading.

m   Rithner, Juan Raul, and others. Aquí, Río Negro cuentos
     rionegrinos. (Buenos Aires: Editorial Plus Ultra, 1979.
     79 p.) Gr. 10-adult.

These thirteen stories and legends were selected
from a literary contest held in Río Negro, Argentina,
so that young readers could be exposed to the literature
of various regions of Argentina.   There is a wide variety
of stories represented in this collection: Some are difficult to read--they describe abstract happenings such as
the formation of lakes and rivers, or they bore readers
with an obvious message: "En esta casa no entrará
nunca la desgracia ... porque los niños saben buscar la
buena suerte trabajando. [Adversity will never enter in
this house ... because children know to look for good
luck through work.]" p. 76.

*   Yalí. Las trampas del Curupí y otras leyendas. (Bue-
     nos Aires: Centro Editor de América Latina, 1976.
     30 p.) Gr. 5-8.

Two lively legends from Argentina are included:
"Las trampas del Curupí, " which tells why Indian mothers in Argentina only are calm and allow their children
to play far away from home while the "Curupí" sleeps;
and "Eireté la indiecita, " which tells how Eireté, a lovely Indian girl, learned how to weave the beautiful "ñan-
dutí" fabric. It is indeed unfortunate that the illustrations do not do justice to these tales; they are blurred
patches of color which lack imagination.

NONFICTION

* Montes, Graciela. <u>Gran enciclopedia de los pequeños.</u>
Illus: Clara Urquijo and others. (Buenos Aires: Editorial La Encima, 1980. [100 p.]) Gr. 5-8.

The title of this book is misleading, as it is not an encyclopedia for young readers but rather an interesting manner of introducing animals to children: First it includes a simple autobiography that highlights important aspects of the animals' lives; then it includes a traditional Argentine legend where the specific animal is the main character; and, lastly, it contains two pages of technical/scientific information about each animal. The animals described in this book are "hornero, " a common bird of Argentina; a fox, a cricket; an armadillo; an anteater; and a toad.
Animal lovers will be delighted with these engaging stories and legends as well as with the amusing illustrations of animals in various situations.

POETRY

m Bacas, Nidia, and Mabel Morvillo. <u>El arcoiris de Ana.</u>
Illus: Amalia Cernadas. (Buenos Aires: Editorial Plus Ultra, 1979. 94 p.) Gr. 3-5.

In fifty-one simple poems Ana tells about her friends, places she knows, games, songs, and mischiefs. Some of these poems could be read out loud to children, as they are lively as well as amusing.
Unsophisticated three-tone illustrations complement most poems.

m Benarós, León. <u>Romances argentinos: historia, leyenda y oficios criollos.</u> (Buenos Aires: Editorial Plus Ultra, 1981. 206 p.) Gr. 9-12.

These poems relate historical episodes or legends from Argentina as well as provide glimpses of the common workers and people of that country. They are written in simple octosyllabic verses, which are easy to read. They tell of shootings of well-known figures, the life of a guitar player, the tragic death of a young woman, and other emotional incidents.

Poetry lovers may enjoy the action and simplicity
of these poems/romances.

m   Breda, Emilio. Los villancicos de Francisco de Asis.
Illus: Adolfo Tanoira. (Buenos Aires: Goyanarte Editor, 1978. 74 p.) Gr. 4-8.

These forty-nine religious poems are meant to glori-
fy the Lord. Some are religious poems about nature in
honor of Christmas Eve, others tell about miraculous
happenings, and others are about animals who came (or
attempted to come) to worship the Lord. The following
is a translated example of a poem about a giraffe who
couldn't make it:

Poem to the Absent Giraffe
Why didn't the giraffe come?
She wanted to wear a necktie
to see her Christ-Child.
The poor thing did not succeed (p. 43)

Two-tone, uninspired illustrations complement each
poem.

m   Domínguez, María Alicia. Canciones de Mari Alas.
Illus: Leticia Uhalde. (Buenos Aires: Editorial Plus
Ultra, 1979. 47 p.) Gr. 2-5.

These twenty-two simple rhymes tell about babies
going to sleep, a naughty girl, a little bird, a green
lizard, a chocolate soldier, flying swallows, a curious
ant, a dream, and other child-like themes. Some of
the rhymes are too childish for fourth and fifth graders
and others contain difficult vocabulary for second and
third graders. Most of the unaffected three-tone illustrations, however, will appeal only to younger children.

nr   Echauri de Estefanía, Elsa. Enanito ... ¿dónde estás?
Illus: Martica. (Buenos Aires: Editorial Plus Ultra,
1981. 48 p.) Gr. 3-5.

This includes twenty-two poems and stories about
things that would interest very young children if they
were written in a simpler language. They tell of a little

duck that likes to sing, a little dwarf who hides in the
forest, a little girl who plays with her doll, a clown, a
pirate, three little kittens, a carnival, a very "good and
well-educated girl" who plays with butterflies, and others.
    The three-tone illustrations are too childish, and the
vocabulary is too complex, making this book inappropriate for younger or older children.

m   Gaiero, Elsa Lira.   Cancionero del duende verde.   Illus:
     Gustavo M. Bech.   (Buenos Aires: Editorial Plus Ultra,
     1980.   47 p.)   Gr. 2-4.

     This is a collection of twenty poems about things
common to children: a green goblin, a turtle's trip, a
golden frog, a giraffe's wedding, three ships, a traveling
cricket, a lonely star, a blond bee, a scarecrow and
others.
     Plain, three-tone illustrations complement each poem.
The simplicity of these poems might appeal to most young
children.

nr   González Lanuza, Eduardo.   El pimpiringallo y otros
     pajaritos.   Illus: Amalia Cernadas.   (Buenos Aires:
     Librería Huemul, 1980.   41 p.)   Gr. 1-3.

     This is a wearisome collection of twenty-two poems
about animals, toys, and flowers that will bore children
with its saccharine rhymes and messages.
     Three-tone lackluster illustrations complement these
insipid poems.

nr   González Luna, Eduardo.   Aires para canciones.   (Bue-
     nos Aires: Editorial Plus Ultra, 1981.   71 p.)   Gr. 9-
     adult.

     Through these poems the author wished to share his
joy of life, which "many times hides under sadness. "
It includes poems from the cradle until death, emphasizing the "luminosity of love. "   I cannot believe that
adolescents will enjoy these overly sentimental poems
about love, God, and nature.   The following is a trans-
lation of a brief poem about faith:

         If you go blindly, then why

the light of your lantern?
--Because of your lack of faith (p. 43)

* Hernández, José. El Martín Fierro para los niños.
(Buenos Aires: Editodos, 1977. 61 p.) Gr. 8-12.

This book contains an excellent adaptation for young
readers of the first part of the famous poem El Gaucho
Martín Fierro. It includes the adventures, struggles,
and sorrows of Martín Fierro in his native Argentina.
It relates his desperate fight against corruption and injustice, as well as his solitude and woeful existence.
Bold illustrations complement the powerful and moving
verses.

m Luján Campos, María Luisa de. Sueños de mentira.
Illus: Diana Akselman. (Buenos Aires: Editorial Plus
Ultra, 1981. 46 p.) Gr. 3-5.

This collection of thirty-seven light-hearted poems
and rhymes may appeal to younger readers. They tell
of animals, clocks, angels, stones, and others in common situations. Colorful illustrations complement each
poem and rhyme.

m Malinow, Inés. Canciones para mis nenas llenas de sol.
Illus: Luis Pollini. (Buenos Aires: Editorial Plus Ultra, 1981. 47 p.) Gr. 2-4.

These thirty-seven simple poems and rhymes may
appeal to younger children who are still interested in
reading about little shoes, dolls, hungry mice, paper
boats, little spiders, and similar topics. Appropriate
bright illustrations accompany each poem and rhyme.

nr Merlino, Carlos Alberto. La luna en bicicleta. Illus:
Gustavo M. Bech. (Buenos Aires: Editorial Plus Ultra,
1981. 47 p.) Gr. 2-4.

These forty inane poems about toys, little trees,
birds, clouds, kittens, and other nature themes lack
reader appeal. The author's grandiose descriptions of
a "wonderful, beautiful humane world" and other simplis-

tic assertions are indeed tiresome to read. The inanimate three-tone illustrations are as dull as the poems.

nr Ocampo, Silvina. Canto escolar. Illus: Guido Bruveris.
    Photos: Jorge Mischkinis. (Buenos Aires: Editorial
    Fraterna, 1979. 75 p.) Gr. 6-8.

    This includes twelve saccharine poems that will an-
    noy young readers with their "proper" messages. They
    describe perfect students who love their country; beauti-
    ful trees that are always friendly; a young girl who likes
    to dream; the author's favorite doll; an unusual mermaid;
    the ideal, patient teacher; the promises that young people
    make to their country; and others. I cannot imagine
    young people reading these poems for any reason. I
    certainly hope they won't.

nr Pitella, Ana María. Cantos, cuentos y versos para
    niños. (Buenos Aires: Ediciones Agon, 1981. 59 p.)
    Gr. 5-7.

    These ten songs, four stories, and fourteen poems
    describe good children, loving mothers, kind fathers,
    sweet grandmothers, the joy of thankful and well-behaved
    children, the dreams of hard-working girls, and other
    tiresome topics. This is certainly not an entertaining
    or appealing book for any reader.

nr Ravagnan de Jaccard, Blanca. Luciana de la sombrilla.
    (Buenos Aires: Libros de América, 1980. 60 p.) Gr.
    4-6.

    This is a collection of forty-one saccharine poems
    about a young girl who played with flowers and umbrellas,
    the wonders of nature, the arrival of summer, well-
    behaved children, and other tepid topics. These poems
    are either too insipid or too affected to appeal to young
    readers.

m   Riva, Myriam. Garabatos de Luliglobito. Illus: Sonia
    Trovato y Gabriel Irvini. (Buenos Aires: Editorial Plus
    Ultra, 1981. 48 p.) Gr. 2-4.

Included here are twenty-two poems that tell about a shoe, the sun, a puppet, a teddy bear, winter, a dog, an onion, eating rice with sticks, and other things common to children. The three-tone illustrations and the simple thoughts expressed in these poems might appeal to some children.

nr Solimando, Felisa de. Bombas y platillos, nietos y sobrinos. Illus: Ernesto Valor. (Buenos Aires: Editorial Plus Ultra, 1979. 71 p.) Gr. 6-8.

These thirty-one poems will certainly not appeal to children for whom they were ostensibly written. In a most affected style, they tell about a loving aunt, Mariana's little bed, a white onion, God, mother's flowers, an old pail, a hard-working grandmother, and others. Stiff, two-tone illustrations complement each poem.

The following is a translated example of one of the poems:

Poetry

A child has asked me:
What is poetry? ...
And I answered:
Poetry is kindness, is tenderness,
Is charity, understanding, and sorrow,
Is joy and perfume of a flower (p. 63)

nr Vettier, Adela. De la mano: poemas y cuentos. (Buenos Aires: Editorial Plus Ultra, 1978. 111 p.) Gr. 9-12.

This collection of poems and a few short stories describes the author's reminiscences of her own adolescence. I wonder if young adults will be interested in reading poems which tell about the author's feelings and thoughts about rain, her younger sister, her childhood, a bird, a fisherman, the sea, and many other highly sentimental memories. A few of the short stories are written in a more natural style, and, consequently, are more interesting to read, such as "Las Cartas de Tío Pablo, " "Navidad en bicicleta, " and "El joven del cuadro. "

The other stories are written in an emotional language which is not interesting to read. The following is from "Valeria del mar": "Venían a buscarme mis sueños, las fantasías ardientemente vividas hasta convertirse en una segunda realidad posible.... Yo sabía ahora que había estado a punto de irme para siempre al mundo que mi fantasía me hizo amar, y que tal vez espera, espera siempre, en el borde mismo de la realidad. [My dreams came to look for me, the fantasies fearlessly lived until they became a second possible reality.... I knew now that I almost left forever to the world that my fantasy made me love, and that perhaps it waits, it waits forever, in the fringe of reality.]" p. 81.

THEATER

nr   Finkel, Berta. El títere y lo titiritesco en la vida del niño. (Buenos Aires: Editorial Plus Ultra, 1980. 158 p.) Gr. 6-adult.

The author's purpose in writing this collection of sixteen puppet plays is to present to young people human passions and feelings "at the child's level ... without exciting him ... thus avoiding all kinds of violence. " In the first forty-five pages the author describes her thoughts about puppets for children followed by sixteen plays and their introductions.
There are plays about animals, a Christmas tree, a traveling musician, a magic litter, and others. Perhaps some adults might be interested in reading about puppetry for children; young readers, however, will be bored by these monotonous plays.

nr   López, Graciela Alicia. Patio criollo. Santiago del Estero: Caro Hnos, 1979. 120 p.) Gr. 6-9.

The purpose of these eighteen plays for children is to introduce them to life in rural Argentina. According to the author, they reflect the humor and tenderness of the people. They are written in the vernacular, hence the long dialogues are very difficult to understand by other Spanish readers. Very few children will be interested in reading plays about new shoes or old people or tedious monologues about the feelings of an old man about his town.

nr   Walsamakis, Olinda de. Silbajando bajito. (Buenos

Aires: Ediciones Tres Tiempos, 1981.   119 p.)   Gr. 5-7.

This is a collection of three plays, four puppet shows, and one poem that will put actors, spectators, and readers to sleep.   The puppet shows are about animals in the forest, a trainer of tigers, children at play, and a rabbit in search of a friend.   The plays are about small animals, a birthday cake, and a swan.   The poem tells about God who paints a beautiful landscape every morning.

The insipid characters and vacuous plots make these plays inappropriate for anyone.

FICTION

m   Montes y Lukas, Hugo. Leyendo a Chile. (Santiago:
Editorial Andrés Bello, 1977. 125 p.) Gr. 9-12.

The purpose of this anthology is to introduce young
readers to the literature of Chile. It includes a historical overview of Chilean literature, beginning with Pedro
de Valdivia's letters. Subsequently, it discusses Alonso
de Ercilla's masterpiece, La Arauca, and the great
poetry of Rubén Darío, Gabriela Mistral, Pablo Neruda,
and Vicente Huidobro. It also mentions the prose works
of Alberto Blest Gana, Baldomero Lillo, Eduardo Ba-
rrios, and Manuel Rojas. In spite of the obvious pedagogical intent of this anthology, it does offer a carefully
selected collection of Chile's literature, with interesting
references to the authors' lives and works.

nr Secretaría de Relaciones Culturales del Ministerio.
Primera antología de poesía y cuento infantil. (Santiago
de Chile: Editorial Universitaria, 1979. 166 p.) Gr.
6-10.

This anthology includes the winners of a National
Contest of Poetry and Stories for Children. There are
ten stories and nine poems represented. The Ministry
of Cultural Relations of Chile should be commended in
their efforts to foster the creation of children's literature; however, these stories and poems will certainly
not appeal to young readers. They are written in a complicated style, many of them with a religious message.
The following is an example of an overly sentimental
paragraph from the story "La Pincoya, " which received

the first prize: "Comenzaba a caminar entonces hacia
la costa, hasta que la arena iba adhiriéndose a sus to-
billos en frágiles anillos inestables que nacían y morían
a medida del trayecto. De vez en cuando recogía huiros
de cochayuyo o trocitos de nacar iridiscente, pero nada
conseguía distraerlo ni alegrarlo. En su interior sentía
una convulsión emotiva a punto de estallar en llanto, que
ya empezaba a nublar la visión de sus pupilas. [He
then started to walk towards the shore, until the sand
started to adhere to his ankles in fragile, fickle circles
which would live and die on the road. Sometimes he
would pick up pieces of iridescent mother-of-pearl, but
nothing could distract him or gladden him. Within him
he felt an emotional convulsion ready to burst in tears,
which had already clouded the vision of his eyes.]" p.
14.

POETRY

nr   Navarro, Rebeca. Poesía de gatos. Santiago: Pontificia
Universidad Católica de Chile, 1979. 32 p.) Gr. 2-4.

This is a collection of twelve poems about cats.
They tell about the life of cats as well as their duties,
wishes, and thoughts. A few of these poems might be
enjoyed by cat lovers, but, unfortunately, the cheap format of this book will not appeal to children. Moreover,
it includes too many obvious typographical mistakes and
blurred, black-and-white illustrations.

COLOMBIA

FICTION

nr Fornaguera, María. <u>La farsa de Porahisí.</u> Illus: Juan
Antonio Roda. (Bogotá: Carlos Valencia Editores, 1980.
94 p.) Gr. 5-8.

These three abstruse fantasy stories about "mechan-
ized society" are impossible to enjoy. The strange sym-
bolism and complicated language of these stories about
convertible ships, an amazing computer, and a mysterious flying horse make them a certain bore. The six
full-page illustrations are static and uninspired.

nr Rodríguez Castelo, Hernán. <u>La historia del fantasmita</u>
<u>de las gafas verdes.</u> Illus: J. Villa. (Bogotá: Círculo
de Lectores, 1978. 95 p.) Gr. 6-8.

This is not a book for children but a dull philosophical discussion about life and death, love and hope, op-
timism and sadness. The main character is a little
ghost and through him the author expounds his protracted
theories about learning human speech. The following is
how the little ghost learned the meaning of the verb "to
love": He overheard a pretty girl saying, "Yo amo a
mi mamá porque es buena. Mi mamá me ama porque
soy pequeña. [I love my mother because she is good.
My mother loves me because I am little.]" p. 30.
There are also endless chapters on the little ghost's
meetings with death, the devil, an angel, and the author's
main preoccupation--resurrection: "Todos los hombres
tienen que morir.... Pero resusitarán.... El sol, re-
cuérdalo. El sol. De la muerte se pasa a la vida,
como de la obscuridad se pasa a la luz cuando sale el

sol. [All men must die.... But they will resurrect....
The sun, remember it. The sun. From death you pass
to life, like from darkness you pass to light when the
sun comes out.]" p. 90, 92. A few small, blurred illustrations complement the pages and pages of lengthy
text.

nr   Vélez, Rubén. Hip hipopótamo vagabundo. Illus: Victoria Paz. (Medellín: Albón, SA, 1981. 125 p.) Gr.
5-7.

These are fifteen tiresome stories about a hippopotamus in various situations: Hip decides to travel; Hip
visits a tower; Hip, a good citizen; Hip in trouble; Hip
in the circus; Hip dreaming; and so forth. A complicated
text with a few illustrations that lack interest.

POETRY

nr   Silva Mojica, Antonio. La niña de las nieves y otros
poemas. Illus: Marcos Guillermo Peñaloza. (Bogotá:
Editorial El Catolicismo, 1980? 48 p.) Gr. 6-8.

Four of these poems deal with topics of interest to
little children--a playful cat, a young calf, two sheep,
hungry birds, a girl and her doll--and the last poem ex-
presses the sad feelings of a boy upon the death of his
sister. Perhaps older readers will be moved by the
last poem, but the first four poems are too long and in-
tricate for young children and too childish for others.

SONGS

m   Fornaguera, María, ed. ¡Que bonito baila el Chulo!
Illus: Lorenzo Jaramillo. (Bogotá: Carlos Valencia
Editores, 1980. [46 p.]) Gr. 2-5.

This is a collection of twenty-one Colombian folk-
songs about animals in various situations. Some of the
illustrations are bright and cheerful and might appeal to
children. Unfortunately, the text is written in colloquial
(Colombian) Spanish, which detracts from its enjoyment
by other Spanish readers. Moreover, it is all written
in cursive, making it difficult to read.

FICTION

nr   Aguiluz, Eva. <u>Había una vez un niño.</u> Illus: Hugo Diaz. (San José: Editorial Costa Rica, 1981. 47 p.) Gr. 6-8.

This is a collection of fourteen brief stories about animals, the sun, the moon, mountains, stars, and other topics which lack interest and action. Black-and-white illustrations of animals and nature complement each story.

nr   Cardona Peña, Alfredo. <u>La nave de las estrellas.</u> (San José: Editorial Costa Rica, 1980. 92 p.) Gr. 5-8.

The author describes this collection of nine stories as "the first science fiction stories written for Costarican children. " Thus, he proceeds to write fantasy stories about a millionaire witch, a poor fairy, a miraculous stork, colorful mice, a palace in the sun, ghosts in the water, and others. Long, tedious descriptions and weak characters make these stories difficult to enjoy.

m   Gutiérrez, Joaquín. <u>Cocorí.</u> Illus: Zdenek Knisk. (San José: Editorial Costa Rica, 1981. 93 p.) Gr. 8-10.

This novel was originally published in Chile in 1947. It tells about Cocorí, a little black boy, who discovers that life can be best lived by doing good things. Cocorí develops a special attachment to a rose who, "in a few hours gave more happiness to others than many others give in years. " Poetically, Cocorí describes his experiences with animals and nature as well as the importance of life.

nr   Herrero Pinto, Floria. El planeta verde. (San José: Editorial Costa Rica, 1980. 48 p.) Gr. 7-9.

This is a fantasy story about Andrus, a young boy, who sets out in search of himself. His father is busy investigating the "great mysteries of the Universe," and Andrus starts his trip among the stars. He then arrives at the home of several witches. Later he finds a piece of paper with "Advice to Be Happy": Sing a song to the moon; tell you secrets to the wind, and others.

At the end of his journey Andrus discovers that he is truly alone in front of the "immensity of the sea." This is an uninteresting story with insipid characters.

*   Leal de Noguera, María. Cuentos viejos. Illus: Osvaldo Salas. (San José: Editorial Costa Rica, 1981. 171 p.) Gr. 6-8.

This is the fifth edition of this well-known collection of twenty-four traditional tales from Costa Rica, originally published in 1938. In a marvelous, simple style Mrs. Noguera relates the adventures of Uncle Rabbit as he outsmarts Uncle Tiger, as well as the undertakings of courageous princes and kind princesses and many others. Unfortunately, the two-tone, trite illustrations do not do justice to the excitement of these tales.

Young children will also enjoy listening to these tales in spite of the homely presentation of this collection.

nr   Morvillo, Mabel. Cuentos con dos cielos y un sol. Illus: Fernando Carballo. (San José: Editorial Costa Rica, 1981. 64 p.) Gr. 5-8.

This is a collection of eight wearisome stories about pencils, love, dreams, a typewriter, and other unremarkable topics. Neither the slow-moving text nor the childish black-and-white illustrations will appeal to young readers.

nr   Sáenz, Carlos Luis. El abuelo cuentacuentos. (San José: Editorial Costa Rica, 1981. 95 p.) Gr. 6-8.

Included here are sixteen stories about animals,
magic hens, fairies, kind old men, understanding grandmothers, and others whose purpose is to entertain as
well as to impart important lessons: "If you are a good
person you will be happy. " "Don't try to accomplish too
much or you will fail. " These stories are much too juvenile for sixth graders and up.

POETRY

nr Sáenz, Carlos Luis. Nido de la canción. (San José:
Editorial Costa Rica, 1981. 84 p.) Gr. 5-8.

These fifty-eight undistinguished poems exhort young
readers to love their country, take care of animals, and
be good. A few lifeless two-tone illustrations are interspersed among the poems.

THEATER

nr Ulloa Z. , Ma. del Rosario. Dramatizaciones infantiles.
(San José: Editorial Costa Rica, 1980. 185 p.) Gr.
5-8.

This is a collection of twenty-seven children's plays
whose purpose is to sensitize young readers/listeners to
the wonders of nature as well as to stimulate in them
"feelings of fraternity, generosity, and admiration. "
Thus, it includes plays which teach children to contem-
plate the beauties of the countryside, to forgive their
enemies, to plant trees, to understand the suffering of
clowns, to appreciate their country, and other admirable
concepts. Obviously, the author forgot to entertain young
readers/viewers; it is hoped that children won't be exposed to such a wearisome collection of "educational"
plays.

FICTION

m   Felipe, Nersys. <u>Román Elé</u>. Illus: Tomás Borbonet.
(La Habana: Casa de las Américas, 1978. 99 p.) Gr.
7-9.

Political messages seem to be very important in
books for young readers published in Cuba. On the first
page the author contrasts the present time "when men
live united and happy, working and resting" with the past
when the "fertile valleys of the Cuyaguateje were full of
servants who worked on the fields and in the houses of
the owners while they [the owners] lived a life of leisure
and wealth" (p. 7). This story tells about the life of
Román Elé, a young, black servant boy, and Cruz María
de los Angeles, the beautiful daughter of the owners of
a large estate ("finca") in Cuba. The children play together and often wish that they could go to school together. The owners obviously disapprove; they also ridi-
cule Román Elé's grandfather because he was going to
take a bath: "¿Quién ha visto que los negros viejos se
bañen?... ¡Ni con todo el jabón del mundo se les quita
la peste que tienen arriba! [Who has seen that old
black men take a bath?... Not even all the soap in the
world will take away the pestilence that they carry!]"
p. 60. Román Elé finally runs away to work at a to-
bacco factory. There he learned that "there are not only
obligations but there are also rights. "
    A few stilted illustrations complement this semi-
political story about life in Cuba before Castro. Perhaps
it may be of interest to young readers to see how even
the arts are used to serve current political thought.

nr Gonzalez, Omar. Nosotros los felices. Illus: Roberto
    Fabelo. (La Habana: Casa de las Américas, 1978.
    71 p.) Gr. 6-10.

    This is a collection of eight short stories with obvi-
ous political messages: crimes committed under the Ba-
tista regime; the success of the Cuban literacy brigades
under Castro; the importance of the military preparation
of young men in Cuba ("Si los Americanos vienen, se-
gurito que se quedan con las ganas de entrar. [If the
Americans come, they will surely keep their wishes to
enter.]" p. 62); and the personal kindness of Fidel Castro.
    One wonders if these stories are meant for internal
or external political propaganda. Surely, Cuban young
readers are not enthralled by the dogmatic plots and
righteous characters in these stories. Readers in other
countries will certainly detect their undisguised intent.

FICTION

m Alvarado, Mario Rodrigo. <u>Paseo gatuno.</u> Illus: E.
Castro. (Quito: Ediciones Colorito, 19?, 14 p.) Gr.
2-4.

 A hungry cat, who often walks the streets at night,
is looking for food and a female companion. He suddenly finds a pretty, female, black cat and love sparks between them. They walk together until they find a trash
can full of garbage, which they call an open-air restaurant. They enjoy their banquet and continue their romantic walk.
 This is an entertaining story with an easy-to-read
text; unfortunately, the illustrations are blurred and disfigured.

m Carrera, Carlos. <u>Cuentos chicos 2.</u> (Quito: El autor,
1978. 119 p.) Gr. 5-7.

 This is a collection of fourteen stories about courageous princes, kind princesses, a playful mouse, the
monster of the blue lagoon, a white swan, and others.
The fast pace and appealing characters of these stories
make them enjoyable reading; it is unfortunate, though,
that they are too difficult to be read by younger children.
The lack of illustrations and very small print make them
inadequate for the potential true readers.

nr _____. <u>El decamerón de los niños.</u> Quito: Editorial
Benalcozar, 1981. 414 p.) Gr. 6-8.

This is an incredibly dull collection of 100 stories
and legends of approximately four pages each which tell
about saccharine animals, benign virgins, patriotic children, and others. Neither the slow-moving stories nor
the unreal characters will appeal to readers of any age.

m   Contreras Navas, Gilberto. La burrita de la abuela:
    cuentos costumbristas americanos. (Quito: Tipografía
    Hispana, 1978.   214 p.) Gr. 10-adult.

    This collection of thirty-four short stories tells about
life in the city and provinces of Ecuador and other South
American countries. Some of these stories criticize the
political situation in South America, others describe
strange happenings, several relate sad love affairs between unsuspecting brothers and sisters, and others recount the experiences of university students. The brevity
and variety of these stories might appeal to young adults
who enjoy fast-paced narratives.

nr Crespo de Salvador, Teresa. Mateo Simbaña. Illus:
    Iñigo Salvador Crespo. (Quito: Consejo Provincial de
    Pichincha, 1981.   34 p.) Gr. 5-7.

    The purpose of this fantasy is to teach Ecuadorean
children that they must protect and love their country--
that they must especially guard against provoking forest
fires. Mateo Simbaña, the young protagonist, suffers
the consequence of a fire started by careless campers.
In this fantasy, Mateo is saved by a condor and taken to
the most beautiful part of the Andes, where he lives in
harmony with nature.
    It is unfortunate that the author confused important
pedagogical objectives with an entertaining story. The
results are a watered-down lesson in fire prevention
and the beauties of nature and a bland story.

*   Icaza, Jorge. Huasipungo para niños. Illus: Ramiro
    Jacome. Adapted by: Juan Otrebor and Jorge Icaza.
    (Quito: Editorial Casa de la Cultura Ecuatoriana, 1978.
    86 p.) Gr. 9-12.

    This is an excellent adaptation for young adults of
the renowned Ecuadorean novel Huasipungo. It is a pow-

erful novel which describes the pain and suffering of the
Indians of Ecuador and their many exploiters: the "mes-
tizo, " the white man, the Church, and the military.
Touchingly, the author narrates how the Indians are de-
prived of their land and their families and are forced to
work under pathetic conditions.   He tells how alcohol is
used by the exploiters as an opium to dull their senses
and continue their exploitation.   He also describes how
the Catholic Church supports the ruling classes and
abuses the trust of the Indians by demanding their hard-
earned savings and threatening them with eternal punishment.

The only disagreeable part of this book is the eight
color illustrations which seem like unfinished tourist-
type scenes of Ecuador.   Otherwise, this is an outstanding adaptation of a poignant and realistic novel.

nr   Paz y Miño Cepeda, María Eugenia. Siempre nunca.
      Cuentos. Illus: Nilo Yépez. (Quito: E P Ediciones,
      1980.   81 p.) Gr. 9-adult.

This collection of nineteen abstruse short stories
covers such topics as death, sickness, solitude, pain,
sadness, and other depressing conditions.   The author's
melancholic writing style and her incessant preoccupation
with human suffering will not appeal to young readers.
Abstract, black-and-white drawings of dejected human
beings illustrate each story.

LEGENDS

*   Movsichoff Zavala, Paulina. El cóndor de la vertiente:
      leyenda salasaca. Illus: Oswaldo Viteri. (Quito: Edi-
      ciones del Sol Cia Ltda, 1978. [24 p.]) Gr. 4-10.

This beautiful pre-Columbian legend from Ecuador
tells how a condor (a large South American vulture)
loved and protected the Salasaca people.   He lived alone
in a huge cavern, but one day he became lonely and took
Mallu Quinche, the prettiest Salasaca maiden, to live
with him.   She was very unhappy, and her parents had
given up all hope of ever seeing her again.   Suddenly,
Mallu Quinche returned home and gave birth to a feath-
ered being--half man and half bird--and died shortly
thereafter.   Since then no unmarried woman goes to the
water spring and the condor is again alone and sad.

Distinctive colorful illustrations add much excitement
to this legend. (Some readers might object to a scene
in which Mallu Quinche is shown bathing nude in the
miraculous spring. It is done in such good taste, however, that only prudish adults will have any cause to object.)

m   Yuguilema L., Angel. Cuentos y leyendas de mi tierra.
    Illus: Angel Yuguilema L. (Riobamba, Ecuador, 1978.
    134 p.) Gr. 6-10.

The author collected, translated, edited, and illustrated this bilingual (Quichua-Spanish) collection of fifteen
traditional stories and legends from Ecuador. He describes himself as a young farmer and an amateur writ-
er and illustrator, who is interested in maintaining the
native language of his country. He therefore collected
this literary folklore from the oral tales he heard from
his grandparents and parents. He explains that the language used in this book is the language used in the country, as his intention is to conserve the oral tradition.
The stories and legends have indeed preserved their lightness and spontaneity. They tell about the adventures of
Uncle Wolf and Nephew Rabbit; three sisters who wished
to marry a king, a butler, and a cook; several farmers
who lived close to the volcano Chimborazo after its erup-
tion; a dead man who returned to visit his widow; and
other entertaining tales.
The author must be commended for compiling these
delightful tales; however, they need to be rewritten if
they are to be enjoyed by young readers. The long,
complex sentences, spelling mistakes, and generally poor
presentation of this book detract from the potential appeal of these tales to young readers.

NONFICTION

nr Artieda, Alfonso. Cochasqui: historia de una civiliza-
    ción destruida. (Quito: Tipografía Hispana, 1978.
    [92 p.]) Gr. 9-adult.

Apparently the small size of this book--3" x 4"--
makes it appear to be a book for young readers. Unfortunately, its unappealing presentation and redundant
text will not entice readers. It includes the author's

personal opinions of why Cochasqui was such an important
civilization: It describes the foundation of the city of
Quitu; the significance of the adoration of the sun, their
god; controversial burial practices; and the issue of
whether or not polygamy existed. The last part of the
book, which discusses the future, includes seven two-
tone photographs which are so blurred that one can barely distinguish their content. Cochasqui deserves a better
history book.

nr   Bianchi, Cesar. El shuar y el ambiente. Illus: Tonino
     Clemente. (Ecuador?: Mundo Shuar, 1981. 270 p.)
     Gr. 9-12.

       In a disorganized and poorly edited manner, this
     book describes the environment in which the Shuars, one
     of the largest ethnic groups of the Amazon, live. It
     tells about their hunting techniques and weapons and
     emphasizes that they only kill the animals they need for
     food. It also includes facts about various types of ani-
     mals as well as some legends and stories that relate
     hunting experiences in the Amazon.
       This book contains lots of information. It is indeed
     unfortunate, though, that it wasn't edited or organized in
     a readable manner; it is too confusing and disjointed.

m   Rodríguez Castelo, Hernán. Como nació el castellano.
     (Quito: Editorial Publitécnica, 1979. 47 p.) Gr. 9-
     adult.

       This book was written in commemoration of the birth
     --one thousand years ago--of the Spanish (Castilian) lan-
     guage. It briefly explains how the Latin language, which
     was spoken in Iberia, was converted into Castilian. It
     also describes the expansion of Castilian to most of the
     Iberian Peninsula. Serious students of the language might
     be interested in this simple attempt to show the growth
     and development of what is now the Spanish language.

NURSERY RHYMES

m   Rivas R, Lcdo. Manual de rondas, canciones escolares
     e himnos. (Guayaquil: La Autora, 1980. 192 p.) Gr.
     3-6.

This is a collection of ninety-two nursery rhymes,
twenty-three hymns, thirty-nine songs, and three poems
for children from Ecuador. Unfortunately, the cheap presentation of this publication and many typographical mistakes, as well as the poor selection of nursery rhymes,
hymns, and songs, make most of this collection unappealing to children. For example, too many of the selec-
tions deal with students' gratitude to their teachers, love
of their country, motherly love, and other concepts that
adults wish to inculcate in children.

POETRY

nr   Crespo de Salvador, Teresa. Hilván de sueños. Illus:
     Bolivar Mena Franco. (Quito: Medina-Aguirre Impre-
     sores, 1978. 30 p.) Gr. 4-6.

     Seven saccharine "poems in prose" about a tree, a
stone, grass, a butterfly, a mirror, a merry-go-round,
and birds which thank God for their existence or the author's own grateful memory for having existed. Neither
the stilted two-tone illustrations nor the pretentious language used in the poems should be exposed to young
readers.

nr   Moreno Heredia, Eugenio. Poemas para niños. Illus:
     Vicente Arevalo. (Quito: Editorial del Ministerio de
     Educación, 1981. 67 p.) Gr. 3-5.

     This is a collection of thirty poems for children
about animals, an apple, a little school, toys, the joy
of living, the beauty of peace, and other saccharine
topics. Some of the poems are too difficult for young
children to understand, and others are too childish for
those children who might be able to read them. The
unattractive format of this publication--cheap paper, one-
tone illustrations--is an additional detriment.

nr   Poesía y relato estudiantil 1981. (Latacunga: Asociación
     de Trabajadores de la Cultura de Cotopaxi, 1981. 31 p.)
     Gr. 9-adult.

     Nine poems and four short stories are included in
this collection of award-winning student works from the
province of Cotopaxi in Ecuador. The purpose of this

contest is to motivate the artistic creation of the students of Cotopaxi. The poems and stories tell about heroes, mothers, wars, beloved towns, depressed writers, impoverished peasants, and passionate love affairs.

The students must be commended for their artistic endeavors, but other young readers will find these poems and short stories melodramatic as well as amateurish. The awkward black-and-white illustrations further detract from this publication.

nr   Vélez V. de Patiño, Gloria A.   Recuerdos infantiles. Illus: Wilson Arteaga Canarte. (Portoviejo: Casa de la Cultura Ecuatoriana Núcleo de Manabí, 1978. 141 p.) Gr. 3-6.

In this collection there are sixty-five poems and sixteen songs that the author believes will appeal to children in grades 1 through 6. They tell about a kind and perfect father, a lovable grandmother, a gentle Jesus Christ, a dear country, a sweet teacher, a loyal school, a heroic flag, and other lofty ideas. The artificial writing style and pretentious concepts advocated in these poems and songs should be hidden from young readers of all ages.

FICTION

m Mafalda. El televisor. Illus: Quinto. (México: Editorial Nueva Imagen, 1979. [28 p.]) Gr. 2-4.

When Mafalda realized that she was the only girl in school who did not own a TV set, she confronted her father: "Los chicos me miran como un bicho raro porque no tengo televisor. [Boys and girls look at me like a strange animal because I do not own a TV.]" Her father worried that Mafalda would spend hours in front of a TV set singing silly commercials. So Mafalda conceived a plan to get her father to buy a TV. Cartoon-like illustrations complement the simple text.

nr Noto, Elisa. El pastorcito y la paloma. Illus: Le Gonz. (México: Federación Editorial Mexicana, 1978. 55 p.) Gr. 5-7.

These four insipid, moralistic stories can be used as examples of how to bore young readers. "El pastorcito y la paloma" describes the adventures of a pigeon in various countries. The pigeon regrets that there isn't "sufficient love and understanding among men" and conveys a message from Mexican children: "Nuestro corazón es grande, y hay amor para todos. [Our heart is big, and there is love for everybody.]" p. 25. "Solecito y lunita" [Little sun and little moon] must take care of the earth. After much jealousy and suffering, little moon learns that "to give, always to give and with love," that is what makes one happy.

The other two stories tell about Beatriz, a little girl who was so good that the little animals of the forest wished to make her the little princess of the forest.

The five undersized, black-and-white illustrations are as lifeless and uninspiring as the stories in this book.

nr   Robles Boza, Eduardo.   Los cuentos del tío Patota.
     Illus: By five children.   (México: Editorial Patria,
     1980.   76 p.)   Gr. 6-8.

In this long and wearisome collection there are six stories that will surely bore all readers.   They tell about the birth of a letter, a nail that wished to become a screw, the life of a poet, the restlessness of a piece of paper, the life of a typewriter, and the origin of the moon goddess.   The illustrations made by children--ages five to thirteen--add some lightness to the otherwise unbearable stories.

nr   Rodríguez Cirerol, Elvia.   El niño y el viejo.   (México:
     La Autora, 1979.   72 p.)   Gr. 9-12.

This is a collection of thirty-five brief dialogues between an old man and a child.   In two, four, or six sentences they discuss war, books, God, love, happiness, the death penalty, and other momentous concepts.
     Perhaps some adults may find these words of wisdom inspiring, but they are definitely not for younger readers.

nr   Zacarías, Mari.   Cuentos para dormir bien.   Illus:
     Ascención Navidad y Leobardo Palacios G.   (México:
     Compañia General de Ediciones, S. A., 1979.   165 p.)
     Gr. 4-6.

These twenty-five stories for children tell about an airplane that lost its wings, a sweet dragon, a judge and his parrot, a dancing elephant, four wise horses, an animal parade, and others.
     These stories are too child-like to appeal to older children and too verbose to appeal to younger children.

LEGENDS

*   Blackmore, Vivien.   El maíz tiene color de oro: leyendas vegetales.   Illus: Susana Martínez-Ostos.   (México:
     Editorial Novaro, 1981.   48 p.)   Gr. 5-10.

This beautiful collection of six Mexican pre-Columbian legends about plants, flowers, and fruits should appeal to most readers. They tell why corn has the color of gold, why each flower has a name, how chocolate candy saved many peasants, and how a simple drink became a strong alcoholic beverage. Exquisite, colorful illustrations complement each legend.

*   Cook de Leonard, Carmen. Los gemelos contra los gigantes. Illus: By the author. (México: Editorial del Valle de México, 1980. [70 p.]) Gr. 6-10.

This story, which was taken from the great Mayan manuscript "Popol Vuh," tells how two twin brothers fought the giants who controlled the earth and thus prepared the earth for future men and women. It shows them using their intelligence and wit to defeat the strong and powerful giants. Colorful pre-Columbian illustrations depict the family of giants, the giants receiving offerings, the brothers fighting the giants, and various other heroic deeds, which the brothers had to perform by orders of "Huracán," Heart of the Sky. This story is a marvelous introduction to the study of the Mayan culture. However, students familiar with pre-Columbian myths and drawings will find these adventures and illustrations much more appealing. Nevertheless, the fast-moving text and excitement of this story should amuse most readers.

m   Corona, Pascuala. Pita, pita, cedacero: cuentos de nanas. Illus: Eduardo Pisarro. (México: Editorial Novaro, 1981? 58 p.) Gr. 6-10.

These five Mexican traditional tales were originally published in 1945 in Cuentos Mexicanos. They tell of a clever young girl who married a king, a young man who lost everything, an orphan girl who married a prince, a miraculous flower, and a wise charcoal-maker who married a princess. Unfortunately, the vocabulary used in these stories is too difficult for younger children, who might enjoy these tales. The colorful illustrations and general presentation are more appropriate for younger children.

*   Hinojosa, Francisco. La vieja que comía gente: leyendas

de espantos. Illus: Leonel Maciel. (México: Editorial
Novaro, 1981. 48 p.) Gr. 6-10.

Included here are four Mexican legends of spirits
and phantoms with spectacular colorful illustrations and
an extertaining text that should appeal to most readers.
It includes legends about a witch who people thought was
married to the devil, a dead nun who returned from the
dead, a courageous giant, and an old woman who ate people.

* _____, and Raúl Navarrete. El sol, la luna y las
estrellas: leyendas de la creación. Illus: Francisco
Toledo. (México: Editorial Novaro, 1981. 48 p.) Gr.
7-10.

These four Mexican pre-Columbian legends tell about
the creation of the earth: How Huitzilopochtli presented
himself to man; how God formed humanity; how rain
comes from the mountain; and how the sun, the moon,
and the stars were formed. Modernistic, abstract illustrations (many of them of nude women) complement the
text.

* Kurtycz, Marcos, and Ana García Kobeh. De tigres y
tlacuaches: leyendas animales. (México: Organización
Editorial Novaro, 1981. 46 p.) Gr. 5-9.

This excellent adaptation of six Mexican legends
about animals will charm readers with their wit and re-
sourcefulness. It includes legends about the marriage
of a hummingbird, the shrewdness of a tiger, the punishment of a bat, the dream of a fly, the stubbornness of
a turtle, and the mistake of a dog. Striking animal illustrations complement each legend.

NONFICTION

m Dultzin Dubin, Susana. Sonidos y ritmos. Illus: Leonel
Maciel. (México: Editorial Patria, 1981. 40 p.) Gr.
3-5.

The purpose of this book seems to be to introduce
young readers to sounds and rhythms. It encourages

them to listen to the sounds around them and to try to
replicate them. It explains that there are loud, unpleasant sounds and nice, pleasurable sounds, and that rhythm
in music is sometimes fast and sometimes slow. Colorful, modernistic illustrations complement the slow-moving
text.

*   Echeverría, Eugenia. Las frutas. Illus: Leonel Maciel.
      (México: Editorial Patria, 1981. 40 p.) Gr. 3-6.

      Delightful introduction to many fruits that are grown
in Mexico. A simple, amusing text and spectacular,
colorful illustrations describe about forty different fruits
emphasizing their special characteristics.

m   Espinosa de Serrano, Amparo. Había una vez mi familia.
      (México: Siglo XXI Editores, 1981. 184 p.) Gr. 10-
      adult.

      One wonders what the purpose of this book is. It
has beautiful color photographs of Mexican children of
various socioeconomic levels. It also includes illustrations by children--ages five to thirteen--of their families
with an accompanying text. Moreover, it includes psycho-
logical explanations of the children's statements and drawings as well as excerpts of well-known Mexican poems.
This is definitely not a book for children but rather a
sociological/psychological study of Mexican children and
their families.

*   Giron, Nicole. El agua. Illus: Felipe Morales. (Méx-
      ico: Editorial Patria, 1981. 36 p.) Gr. 3-5.

      The importance of water in rural Mexico is depicted
through a simple text and colorful illustrations. It emphasizes the significance of conserving water and of using
water for farming, for producing electricity, and for
bathing and washing. Some readers might object to two
scenes: a nude woman bathing in a river and a nude
boy fishing for carp.

*   _____. El mar. Illus: Leonel Maciel. (México:
      Editorial Patria, 1981. 44 p.) Gr. 3-5.

Life by the sea is simply described in this easy-to-read book. It tells about the vastness of the ocean, the beauty of marine life, the excitement of fishing, and other activities. The modernistic water-color illustrations add animation to the story, even though they are too vague to be informative.

* Hiriart Urdanivia, Berta. Los títeres. Photography by: Marie-Cristine Camus. (México: Editorial Patria, 1981. 40 p.) Gr. 3-5.

A young girl describes her life with her family: They make puppets and produce puppet shows for children. A simple text and excellent color photographs show the family at work making puppets, writing stories, setting up a show, and various other activities involved in producing a puppet show for children.

nr Jacob, Esther. Un pueblo unido, jamás será vencido (lo que pasó en Nicaragua no es un cuento). Illus: Myriam Holgado. (México: Editorial Nueva Imagen, 1980. 50 p.) Gr. 6-10.

This book has strong political messages: to show young readers the abuses and corruption of the Somoza regime in Nicaragua, the love for freedom and justice of the Sandinistas, and U. S. involvement in Nicaragua. It is written in simple but passionate language with black-and-white drawings which emphasize "the people's rights to fight for freedom and justice. " It depicts the vast differences in social/economic classes which prevailed in Nacaragua during the Somozas' regimes, as well as the revolutionary war which finally overthrew the last Somoza dictator. The political message is strongly emphasized on the last page when it reminds young readers that this war occurred in Nicaragua: "Pero todos deben recordarla. Para tener más fuerza. Para poder cuidar y defender siempre a su patria.... Esta historia es también esperanza para otros pueblos oprimidos. [But all must remember it. To become stronger. To be able to always guard and defend your country.... This history is also hope for other oppressed countries]" p. 50.

* Urrutia, Cristina, and Marcial Camilo. El maíz. Illus:
Marcial Camilo. (México: Editorial Patria, 1981. 44
p.) Gr. 3- 5.

    Life in rural Mexico is beautifully described through
the planting, harvesting, and cooking of corn. Stunning,
water- color illustrations and a simple text show how corn
is grown, life in a village, celebrating a good harvest,
working on the fields, and many other activities related
to the eating and growing of corn in Mexico.

POETRY

* Gerez, Toni de. Mi canción es un pedazo de jade:
poemas del México antiguo. Illus: Guillermo Stark.
(México: Editorial Novaro, 1981. 48 p.) Gr. 6- 10.

    This is an outstanding collection of Nahuatl poems
from pre- Columbian Mexico that have been beautifully
adapted/translated by Toni de Gerez with striking pre-
Columbian-type illustrations. This is an excellent introduction to pre- Columbian culture, gods, and literature
which will interest most readers with its splendid thoughts
and wisdom.

PERU

NONFICTION

m De la Jara, Victoria. <u>Historia del antiguo Perú escrita</u>
<u>para niños.</u> Illus: Lorenzo Osores. (Lima: Instituto
Nacional de Cultura, 1978. 15 p.) Gr. 8-12.

This brief publication with beautiful pre-Columbian
illustrations narrates the origin of the Inca empire, the
migration of the Ayars, and the importance of Mama
Waku as a diviner. Unfortunately, this is not, as the
title mistakenly indicates, a history of old Peru, but
rather a series of unconnected narratives, which do not
do justice to the exciting history of Peru.

FICTION

nr Aboy Valldejuli, Carmen. Cucuyé. Illus: Poli Marichal. (Puerto Rico: Empresas Cucuyé, 1979. [46 p.])
Gr. 3-5.

   This is a collection of four saccharine stories that
tell about Cucuyé, a little fairy, and his magical adventures in an enchanted forest; Cucuyé and the tiny princess
"Chiquitina"; Cucuyé, the champion cowboy; and Cucuyé
and the dragón with red eyes. The long descriptions of
Cucuyé's magical adventures lack interest and excitement.
The illustrations are more appropriate for younger children, and the text is a sure bore for any reader.

nr _____. Cucuyé en la cocina. Illus: Poli Marichal.
(Puerto Rico: Empresas Cucuyé, 1980. [13 p.]) Gr.
3-6.

   Cucuyé, the kind fairy, was sad because his friends
could not afford new pairs of boots. His fairy godmother told him of a cooking contest in which the first
prize would be money. He got together with his friends
to experiment in the kitchen. Most of the things they
tried did not taste very good until they tried mama's
favorite recipe. Because they worked so diligently,
their cakes were a complete success, and they won the
first prize. Hence, the poor fairies got their new boots.
The obvious moral of this story and the long text result
in dull reading. Only the gay, colorful illustrations will
appeal to young children.

m _____. Cucuyé y el gigante inocentón. Illus: Poli

Marichal.   (Puerto Rico: Empresas Cucuyé, 1980.   [13 p.])   Gr. 3-5.

A good and inoffensive giant couldn't understand why the children in fantasyland would not play with him.   He was sad and lonely until Cucuyé, a brave little boy, decided to do something about it.   Cucuyé approached the giant and encouraged all the children in town to do likewise.   The good giant became the town's hero when a bad giant--who wished to destroy the town--was defeated by the good giant.   This is a simple story with a very complicated text; hence, it is too difficult to read by younger children who might enjoy reading about "good" and "bad" giants.   The illustrations are appropriate for younger children.

nr   .   Cucuyé y las maravillas del mar.   Illus: Poli Marichal.   (Puerto Rico: Empresas Cucuyé, 1980. [13 p.])   Gr. 3-6.

Cucuyé, a kind fairy, asks his fairy godmother to help him plan a visit to the bottom of the ocean.   There he sees thousands of fish; a huge whale; Neptune, the King of the Ocean; beautiful mermaids; an octopus; a big turtle (that spent its time reading books); and other marvels of the sea.
This is a slow-moving story with two underlying messages: read books and listen to your teachers. Neither the long, tedious descriptions nor the educational messages will appeal to young readers.

nr   Chiesa, Carmen.   Príncipe.   Illus: Aida Busó Negrón. (Rio Piedras: Carmen Chiesa, 1980.   117 p.)   Gr. 7-10.

Through the autobiography of a dog, Príncipe, the author wished to portray the ugliness in this world. Thus, the reader is exposed to the hunger of poor people, the suffering of lepers, the injustices and hypocrisy of society, and finally the death of Príncipe.   Fortunately, the Lord cared and guided Príncipe to his short-lived happiness on this earth.   Eleven melancholic poems written in tribute to Príncipe make up the second part of this book.
Not even dog lovers will be moved by this sociological/novelistic indictment of society.

LEGENDS

m Diaz Marrero, Andrés. La profecía del coquí. Illus:
Sonia Hernández. (Puerto Rico: Editorial Sendero,
1980. 24 p.) Gr. 4-6.

Why the well-known Puerto Rican "coquí" (small
frog) was named "coquí" is simply narrated in this unattractive publication. The awkward, black-and-white
illustrations and the cheap paper certainly detract from
the legend of the Indian mother who gratefully named the
"coquí" for saving her and her baby from well-armed
Spanish "conquistadores." It is hoped that a more appealing version of this legend will be available for young
readers to enjoy.

nr Quiñones, Samuel R. El niño Huamay. Illus: Wilfredo
García. (Puerto Rico: Taller Gráfico Gongoli, 1980?
[14p.]) Gr. 6-9.

This is a sad attempt to reproduce the Taíno legend
that tells about the boy Huamay who is waiting at the top
of the mountain Yuke for the brave warriors to help him
complete his mission--to liberate the Taínos from the injustices they suffered. The text is so difficult to read
and understand that it will surely discourage young readers. Moreover, it includes so many Taíno words that
it adds to its complexity. Inexplicably, the vocabulary
at the end of the book is not in alphabetical or any other
logical order. It includes many of the Taíno words used
in the text, but one has to search through three pages of
randomly listed words to find the definition of the word
one is looking for. The clumsy black-and-white illustrations and cheap format of this publication further detract
from its appeal.

POETRY

nr Díaz Marrero, Andrés. Poemas para niños. Illus:
Jorge Luis Morales and others. (Puerto Rico: Andrés
Diaz Marrero, 1979. 36 p.) Gr. 2-5.

This is a collection of eleven uninspired poems for children about a doll, mother, snail, hat, butterfly, little rabbit,
hen, and other animals. Neither the stark black-and-white
illustrations nor the bland poems will appeal to children.

SPAIN

BIOGRAPHY

* León, María Teresa. <u>Cervantes, el soldado que nos</u> <u>enseñó a hablar.</u> (Madrid: <u>Altalena Editores, 1978.</u> <u>195 p.</u>) Gr. 9-adult.

This is an outstanding biography of the great Spanish author Miguel de Cervantes Saavedra. In a most readable and interesting manner the author relates important episodes of Cervantes' life. She also sensitively inserted many quotes from Cervantes' most popular works, making this biography a beautiful introduction to Cervantes' literary production. It includes Cervantes' life as a poor student, as a soldier, as a captive in Algiers, as a misunderstood husband, as a prisoner in Seville, as an author, and as the unsuccessful Quijote in search of his ideals. Discreetly, the author alludes to Cervantes' love life and to other aspects of his life that are not well known. Moreover, the author succeeds very well in describing life in Spain during Cervantes' lifetime, as well as crucial moments of history which precipitated Spain's downfall, such as the defeat of the Spanish Armada. Modernistic black-and-white drawings of Cervantes add a special mood to the text.

FICTION

* Alcantara Sgarb, Ricardo. <u>La bruja que quiso matar</u> <u>el sol.</u> Illus: María Rius. (Barcelona: Ediciones <u>Hymsa,</u> 1981? 32 p.) Gr. 3-6.

Afkitán was an evil witch who didn't have any friends. She wanted to hurt everyone, but what she hated the most

were the sun and water.   The animals of the forest got
together to fight Afkitán.   They selected a humble goose
to save the sun and water and frighten the terrible witch.
Exquisite animal illustrations and a lively text make this
story delightful reading.

nr   Alibés i Rieta, M. Dolors.   Tres embrollos y una vaca.
      Illus: Rita Culla.   (Barcelona: LaGalera, S. A. , 1981.
      54 p.)   Gr. 4-6.

         Nico, a young boy who likes to write stories is left
      in charge of a cow.   With one hand he types three ani-
      mal stories; with the other he holds the rope that is
      tied to the cow's neck.   He tells of a housefly from Saba-
      dell and how he finally grants it its freedom, of a swal-
      low that came from nowhere, and of a glowworm that
      loved to travel.
         These slow-moving animal stories will bore young
      readers.

nr   Alonso, Fernando.   El duende y el robot.   Illus: Ulises
      Wensell.   (Valladolid: Editorial Miñón, 1981.   79 p.)
      Gr. 6-8.

         A fairy and an intelligent robot meet in the forest
      and become good friends.   The fairy doesn't agree with
      the robot's values and concepts about beauty, so he de-
      cides to teach him "how to think, how to be happy, and
      how to love everybody. "   After long discussions about
      life and beauty, the robot admits that he has learned how
      to appreciate beauty.   They then go around the world
      teaching others "how to have hope" and "be happy":
      "Tienen que visitar todos los pueblos del mundo llevando
      la alegría.   Tienen que trotar todos los caminos de Dios.
      [They must visit all the towns in the world taking happi-
      ness.   They must trot all the journeys to God.]"   p. 76.
         The only appealing thing in this book are the amusing,
      two-tone illustrations.

nr   _____ .   El hombrecillo de papel.   Illus: [by the au-
      thor].   (Valladolid: Editorial Miñón, 1978.   [32 p.])
      Gr. 1-3.

         One spring day a little girl was bored at home so

she designed a child-sized paper man cut out of news-
paper with whom she played all morning. In the afternoon the little man played with her friends and told them
sad stories about war, world catastrophes, and misery.
The children cried, and the little man became sad. The
little man then found a way to talk to the children about
"all the good people that work for others so that our
lives can become better, more just, freer, and more
beautiful. "

Neither this little paper man nor this story will appeal to children due to its obvious educational intent and
dull plot.

m   Amo, Montserrat del.   Excavaciones Blok.   Illus: Rita
      Culla.   (Barcelona: Editorial Juventud, SA. , 1979.
      167 p.)   Gr. 5-8.

      An archaeology professor and three college students
are excavating near the homes of the "Bloks, " four young
boys and girls who often play together.   Because of the
seriousness of the findings, the Bloks are discouraged
from playing at the excavation site by the professor.
However, as the work progresses, the Bloks notice that
there are too many unexplained mysteries, and they decide to investigate.   By carefully observing all clues,
they deduce who could be the thief of the valuable archae-
ological pieces, and in a masterful setup they force him
to accept his dishonesty.   The Bloks are proud of having
discovered the thief; furthermore, they find a way of
keeping an important sculpture in a new museum close
to their own neighborhood.
      This story has amusing dialogues; however, I am
afraid it contains too much archaeology to be enjoyed by
children.   Older students will find the Bloks too childish.
The black-and-white line illustrations are amusing and
witty.

nr   _____.   El nudo.   Illus: María Rius.   (Barcelona:
      Editorial Juventud, 1980.   94 p.)   Gr. 9-12.

      "El nudo" (The knot) is a two-page message to young
readers which encourages them to write in twelve blank
pages "the knot which ties human beings--man or woman. "
It tells them to reaffirm a personal desire or to overcome a difficulty.   The other two stories are equally

abstract. One tells about how a singing mountain avoided war between a well-equipped army and a brave and courageous tribe. The other describes the adventures of three young, valiant mountain climbers and their amazing discovery of a man from outer space who "is strengthened by love and paralyzed by distrust."

The author is too preoccupied with her "important" messages. She neither entertains young readers nor involves them with her excessive moralizing.

m _____. Soñando mar. Illus: Angeles Ruiz de la Prada. (Madrid: Editorial Miñón, 1981. 60 p.) Gr. 5-8.

Three boys from Villacampos--a small town in the center of Spain--fantasize about life by the sea. First, one of their close friends leaves town with his parents to live in Barcelona. They are anxiously waiting for a letter from him, but it never arrives. Then they decide to send a message in a sealed bottle which would travel by river and arrive somewhere in Europe. To their surprise, a few months later, a boy from Portugal sends them a beautiful gift. This story includes realistic descriptions of life in a small town in Spain. Otherwise, it lacks well-drawn characters or enough action to entertain young readers.

* _____. Zuecos y naranjas. Illus: Asun Balzola. (Barcelona: La Galera, 1981. 54 p.) Gr. 4-8.

Vicente, a young Spanish boy, attends a new school in Denmark. There he meets Danish boys and girls who speak a language that he cannot understand. Knud, a Danish boy, is engrossed in drawing Vikings and wishes to teach Vicente how to draw Vikings, but Vicente wants to draw a bullfight--not Vikings. The two boys become good friends when Vicente gives Knud an orange for dessert. (Fresh oranges are special treats in Denmark.) Later Knud notices that Vicente loves his "zuecos" (wooden shoes worn in Denmark) and gives him one in school and takes the other one to his home after school. Vicente's oranges are an instant success with all his classmates, even though Vicente's father misunderstood the nature of his "business."

The excellent characterizations of Vicente and his
father and the amusing exchange of oranges and "zuecos"
make this enjoyable story of a boy in a strange country
a delightful reading experience. Furthermore, the author's natural and simple writing style will appeal to
young readers.

nr   Armijo, Consuelo.   Aniceto, el venececanguelos.   Illus:
     Margarita Puncel.   (Madrid: Ediciones SM, 1981.
     157 p.) Gr. 5-8.

This is a confusing story about Aniceto, a boy who
is afraid of confronting himself.   He gets in trouble at
home, at school, with his aunt and uncle, and with his
friends.   After twenty-one tedious chapters, he realizes
that he must confront his own actions, that he must par-
ticipate in life, and thus he will start becoming a man.
     Neither Aniceto's "difficulties" nor his "solution"
will appeal to young readers.

nr   _____.   Los batautos hacen batautadas.   Illus: Al-
     berto Urdiales.   (Madrid: Espasa-Calpe, S. A. , 1981.
     129 p.) Gr. 5-7.

Included here are thirteen senseless adventures of
"batautos"--original beings with green ears on top of
their heads and green feet--who lived in a remote forest.
They tell of what happened the 42nd day of September,
Peluso's flying kite, Peluso's ragged socks, the longest
walk in the forest, a water-drinking party, a band of
red cabbage, and other "extraordinary" happenings.
     These "adventures" lack humor as well as interest;
they are difficult to read by younger children and ludicrous for older children.

nr   _____.   Macarrones con cuentos.   Illus: Clara Perez
     Escriva.   (Madrid: Emiliano Escolar Editor, 1981?
     91 p.) Gr. 5-7.

Miriam and Rodrigo are invited to eat at their grandmother's house on Sunday.   They eat custard, drink soda
water, and for dessert they have "macaronis with stories. "
Eight difficult-to-read, childish stories about a "good"
pair of boots, an air excursion, a surprise cake, a pirate

who would not shine his own shoes, a king and a donkey, two rabbits and red poppies, and a woman and a cape.

These slow-paced stories with minute black-and-white line illustrations will not interest fifth-to-seventh graders, nor will they appeal to younger children, even if they could read them.

m   . Más Batautos. Illus: Jordi Ciuró. (Barcelona: Editorial Juventud, S. A. , 1978. 70 p.) Gr. 5-7.

This is the second book about "Batautos"--original beings with green ears on top of their heads and green feet. Some "Batautos" are bright and some are stupid, and there is also a crazy one. It includes fifteen stories of approximately four to six pages each in which the author narrates the "Batautos' " witty experiences, such as the morning Peluso had hot chocolate for breakfast at five of his friends' homes, the day Peluso and Buu decided to discover Asia, the time Don Ron organized a big ball at his home, and other stories. Unfortunately, it includes very few illustrations, and some of the stories are a little long and monotonous.

m   . Mercedes e Inés o cuando la tierra gira al revés. Illus: Carmen Andrada Riosalido. (Barcelona: Editorial Noguer, 1981. 189 p.) Gr. 5-8.

This fantasy story describes the adventures of Mercedes, a semi-witch, and Inés, an eight-year-old girl. Mercedes can travel on a broom, by helicopter, or in an automatic taxi, and her main interest is getting magic chick-peas, which she uses to fight firemen, school teachers, or children who don't believe she can do fantastic things. Long, witty descriptions tell about Mercedes and Inés enjoying a strange party in a palace, at a fair, at school, in space, shopping, at a birthday party, and other strange places. Unfortunately, this story is much too long and complicated for young children who might enjoy reading about fantastic people and places. Moreover, the black-and-white line illustrations are too small and perplexing.

*   . El Pampinoplas. Illus: Antonio Tello. (Madrid: Ediciones, S. M. , 1979. 98 p.) Gr. 4-8.

Poliche, who is approximately twelve years old, spends an unforgettable summer vacation with his grandfather in the country. They get involved in innumerable adventures such as building a home-made bicycle, exploring dangerous territory, persecuting the town's thief, organizing a party for grandfather's childhood friends, and other exciting and fun activities. Unfortunately, there are only eight black-and-white illustrations, but the simple, light-hearted text is indeed a joy to read.

nr   Balzola, Asun. Marta y Antón. (Madrid: Edic. Encuentro, 1980? 21 p.) Gr. 2-4.

Marta and Antón live in a beautiful town. In the morning Antón opens the window and sees the birds in the sky and the flowers and plants. Marta hides behind a tree and tells Antón that the mountain is far and the tree is near. There are also flowers, animals, and Mother who came from the store. Finally, Marta and Antón go to bed at night until the next day. This is a dull story with numb illustrations.

m   _____. Pepón y Pepín. (Madrid: Edic. Encuentro, 1980? 20 p.) Gr. 2-4.

Pepón, a giant, and Pepín, a little boy, became good friends. Together they built a home, collected fruit, and ignored the townspeople who made fun of them. When a storm hit the town, Pepín asked Pepón to serve as a bridge to save the people. Everybody loved Pepón after that, and Pepín took care of Pepón's cold.
The simple text and illustrations make this story easy to read.

*   Baquedano, Lucía. Cinco panes de cebada. (Madrid: Ediciones S. M. , 1981. 175 p.) Gr. 9-12.

Muriel is twenty-one years old and anxious to start her new career as a school teacher in Beirechea, a remote town in Spain. Her life in Beirechea is a sharp contrast to her comfortable city life. The school house is a complete disaster, the townspeople seem to ignore her, and she can't even get a list of the children who should attend school. Gradually, and through the patience

and understanding of the town's priest, she begins to
adapt and even to enjoy her work. Her social life also
became more satisfying when she meets several young
women and men her own age. Muriel's commitment to
teaching increases with time as well as her feelings
about the town that she first found so backwards and in-
hospitable. Javier, the town's strangest bachelor, is a
kind and helpful young man. Eventually Javier and Muriel decide they love each other and their town.

Muriel's feelings regarding her life as a teacher, as
well as her personal emotions of loneliness and happiness,
are genuine. In addition the author has done an excellent
job of depicting life in a small farming town in Spain.

*   Calders, Pere. Cepillo. Illus: Carme Solé Vendrell.
     (Barcelona: Ediciones Hymsa, 1981. 24 p.) Gr. 3-5.

When a young boy realized that his mother was going
to give the family's dog away because it had eaten his
father's hat, he searched for a new companion. Finally
in the attic he found an old brush. He tied a rope to
the brush and thus pretended that he owned a strange
dog. "Brush" followed him everywhere, and at night he
noticed that "Brush" moved like a dog. His mother and
father wouldn't believe him, until one night when a thief
came into the house, and "Brush" ran to save his father.
So, "it is not sure that it is, but he may very well be."

Attractive, colorful illustrations complement this
touching story about a boy and his "dog."

nr   Canela Garayoa, Mercè. Eloy, un día fue música. Illus:
     Joan Antoni Poch. (Barcelona: La Galera, S. A., 1981.
     54 p.) Gr. 6-8.

Eloy, a young, curious boy, falls into the tuba of a
visiting musician. There he learns about the life of
musical notes as well as about singers and other musicians. He tries to get out, but he cannot. He finally
manages to get out when the tuba player starts playing
old melodies.

This is a most wearisome fantasy story.

m   _____. Utinghami, el rey de la niebla. Illus: Mont-
     serrat Brucart. (Barcelona: La Galera, 1979. 117 p.)
     Gr. 6-8.

Eulalia lives in a town where everybody is sad since a wicked witch has stolen the light of the imagination. Utinghami, the king of the fog, convinces Eulalia to search for it. With the king's magical powers, Eulalia embarks on a fantasy trip. First they solve the mystery of a powerful king's headaches; then they end up in the bottom of the ocean where a dragon takes again "the light"; and finally, through Eulalia's friendship with a circus gymnast, she obtains the marvelous light of the imagination. Thus, Eulalia is able to give back the imagination to all the children in her class.

This is a well-written fantasy which might be enjoyed by good readers. The subject matter might appeal to younger children, but it is definitely written for older children--the vocabulary and sentence construction are more appropriate for readers from the sixth to the eighth grades.

* Capdevila, Juan. Nico y Ana en el campo. Illus: Violeta Denou. (Barcelona: Editorial Timun Mas, 1979? 28 p.) Gr. K-3.

Simple text and charming illustrations describe Nico's and Ana's visit to a farm. The farmer takes them for a ride in a tractor. They also play in the orchards, collect freshly laid eggs, eat home-made bread and cheese, and for dessert they get a sweet and refreshing watermelon. They return home with many gifts for the family: fruits, vegetables, hens, and a duck. Delightful story about life on a farm.

* _____. Nico y Ana hacen fotos. Illus: Violeta Denou. (Barcelona: Editorial Timun Mas, 1979? 28 p.) Gr. 1-3.

Nico and Ana decide to learn about photography. They watch a photographer at work at a wedding, at a fashion show, at a portrait studio, at a ballet academy, and at a soccer game. The photographer teaches them how to take their own pictures. They also learn to work in the lab. The simple text and charming illustrations will certainly delight young readers and will entice them into the world of photography.

*   . Nico y Ana quieren ser bomberos.   Illus:
Violeta Denou. (Barcelona: Editorial Timun Mas, 1979?
28 p.) Gr. K-3.

When the stove at Nico and Ana's kitchen catches
fire, they call the firemen and decide to become firefighters.   They are introduced to the work of firefighters
by watching them in their daily training exercises, by
accompanying them to extinguish a fire aboard a ship and
at a forest.   They also assist an artist whose house was
flooded and some neighbors whose house was on fire.
They demonstrate how much they've learned by rescuing
a neighbor's cat from a roof.   Simple text and attractive
illustrations introduce young readers to firefighters and
their work.

*   . Nico y Ana quieren ser médicos.   Illus:
Violeta Denou. (Barcelona: Editorial Timun Mas, 1979?
28 p.) Gr. 2-4.

At a picnic with their family, Nico and Ana fall from
a tree and must be taken to a nearby hospital.   After
they are treated for minor injuries, they begin to think
that it must be a good thing to cure people.   Nico walks
through the hospital, and a young doctor invites him to
watch an operation.   They play doctor games and go to
the university to visit the School of Medicine.   Upon returning home, they see a dog with a broken leg and decide to cure him.   They are happy with their first pa-
tient.   Simple text and attractive illustrations introduce
young readers to the world of doctors.

*   . Nico y Ana quieren ser músicos.   Illus: Violeta Denou. (Barcelona: Editorial Timun Mas, 1979?
28 p.) Gr. 1-3.

Simple text and amusing illustrations tell about Nico
and Ana's introduction to the world of music and musicians.   They are shown performing at a school concert,
enjoying the town's band at a city square, listening to an
orchestra at a concert hall, visiting opera singers back
stage, and attending their first music lessons at the
conservatory.   Young readers will enjoy this introduction
to musicians and their work.

*   . <u>Teo en el circo.</u>   Illus: Violeta Denou.
(Barcelona: Editorial Timun Mas, 1977.   28 p.)   Gr.
1-3.

The circus arrives in town and Teo and his friends
go to watch the preparations.   They play with the animals, and they observe various acrobats during their
training.   When the program begins, they are delighted
with an elephant show, acrobats, white horses, magicians, gymnasts, and finally clowns.   Gay, colorful circus illustrations complement the simple text.

*   . <u>Teo en la escuela.</u>   Illus: Violeta Denou.
(Barcelona: Editorial Timun Mas, 1977.   28 p.)   Gr.
1-3.

Teo is shown at school, where he is involved in
various activities such as art classes, physical education,
lunch time, rest time, music lessons, a field trip to a
museum, and a puppet show.   Simple text and colorful
illustrations depict children in a school setting in a most
enjoyable manner.

*   . <u>Teo en la nieve.</u>   Illus: Violeta Denou.
(Barcelona: Editorial Timun Mas, 1977.   28 p.)   Gr.
1-3.

Amid happy winter scenes, Teo describes his skiing
experiences with his friends and teachers.   They are
shown arriving at a winter cottage, spending an evening
by the fireplace, playing in the snow, making a snowman,
learning to ice skate, going for a sleigh ride, and skiing
down a big mountain.

*   . <u>Teo y su familia.</u>   Illus: Violeta Denou.
(Barcelona: Editorial Timus Mas, 1977.   28 p.)   Gr.
1-3.

Teo and his family get ready for Christmas vacation
which they will spend with his grandparents, aunts, uncles,
and cousins.   Colorful illustrations and a simple text
show papa at work at his bakery, mama caring for baby,
Teo setting the table while papa fixes dinner, and finally
all the family getting ready for the trip to the country to
celebrate Christmas.

nr   Chozas, Mercedes. Palabras de cuento. Illus: Jose
      Antonio Diez Rodriguez. (Valladolid: Editorial Minon,
      1980. 48 p.) Gr. 5-7.

      In this collection there are five absurd stories that
tell about Lucas and his decision to eat all the words;
a radio that emitted sounds which looked like worms; a
hairpin that argued with a chick-pea; a chair that never
stopped talking; and the problems of a broom that belonged to a witch.
      These stories are dull as well as senseless. The
black-and-white illustrations are a vain attempt to add
humor to humorless stories.

nr   Conde, Carmen. Doña Centenito, gata salvaje: el libro
      de su vida. Illus: Carlos Torres. (Barcelona: Edi-
      ciones 29, 1979. 48 p.) Gr. 5-7.

      Doña Centenito, an intelligent and sensitive cat, gets
involved in many adventures and philosophical discussions
from an early age. She was born in the forest, and ad-
mires the beauty of nature in the spring. She meets
many friends and is finally captured by a sweet and tender girl.
      This story is too difficult to be read by young chil-
dren who might be interested in a cat's adventures--es-
pecially when it asks questions such as "what are men?"
and "who is better: man or woman?" Older children
will not enjoy reading the saccharine descriptions of
"sweet animals with kind hearts. " The colorful illustrations of animals in the forest are appropriate for
young children only.

*   Fuertes, Gloria. El dragón tragón. Illus: Sanchez
      Muñoz. (Madrid: Editorial Escuela Española, 1979.
      [44 p.]) Gr. 4-6.

      These six witty stories with delightful colorful illus-
trations tell about a dragon that was fed up with pho-
tographers, an octopus that wanted to be a secretary as
he could type and write very fast, a cat from Madrid
that found a home for thirty-three other cats, a small
river that became a lake, a little girl who was never
afraid, and a magic string of garlic that made wonders
for children in school. The author's appealing writing

style and sense of words make these stories especially
attractive for reading out loud. The following is an example of Don Nico's reaction when he found out that
someone had stolen his garlic:

"¿Cómo que no? ¡Mis ajos! ¡Me han robado
mis ajos! ¡Robo y neto asesinato! ¡Me han dejado
sin cabeza! ¡Y sin dientes! ¡de ajo! ¡mis ajos!
¿Dónde estarán mis ajos?"

nr   García Domínguez, Ramón. Un grillo del año dos mil
y pico. Illus: Javier González Solas. (Valladolid:
Miñón, S. A. , 1981? 111 p.) Gr. 5-8.

Slow-moving fantasy story about children in the
twenty-fifth century, which the author wrote when he
realized that city people "are forgetting the country. "
The children in this story had never seen a cauliflower,
or a river, or a horse, or a fruit tree, or a corn field,
or a wheat field; hence, the whole city was terrified
with the appearance of a cricket. Neither the bland
characters nor the vacuous plot will interest young readers.

*   García Sánchez, José Luis, and Miguel Angel Pacheco.
El cocodrilo. Illus: Nella Bosnia. (Madrid: Ediciones
Altea, 1979. 21 p.) Gr. K-3.

Amusing illustrations and a simple text tell about the
life and special characteristics of a crocodile. Young
readers will be delighted with the witty situations in
which the crocodile is shown: brushing its sixty-five
teeth, selecting its food at the grocery store, confronting
a store salesman with a display of crocodile products,
and also basic facts about crocodiles.

*   _____, and _____. La jirafa. Illus: Nella Bosnia. (Madrid: Ediciones Altea, 1979. 18 p.) Gr. K-3.

Humorous illustrations and a simple text tell about
the giraffe. Their height allows giraffes to discover
enemies from a great distance and to eat from the tallest
trees. Giraffes are also shown standing to go to sleep
in a sleeping railroad car, going to a hospital to have a
baby, and baby giraffes running a few hours after birth.

*   _____, and _____. El lobo. Illus: Nella Bosnia.
(Madrid: Ediciones Altea, 1979. 21 p.) Gr. K-3.

Charming illustrations and a simple text tell about
the life and special characteristics of a wolf. Young
readers will enjoy the witty situations in which a wolf
is shown: going out at night to the opera after he rests
during the day, getting together with his friends in winter
to go hunting, running ahead of a group of athletes,
learning to play chess, and also basic facts about wolves.

*   _____, and _____. El tigre. Illus: Nella Bos-
nis. (Madrid: Ediciones Altea, 1979. 21 p.) Gr. K-
3.

Delightful illustrations and a simple text tell about
the life and special characteristics of a tiger. Young
readers will enjoy the witty situations in which a tiger
is shown: eating steak at a fancy restaurant, showing
off its elegant fur, winning medals for being such a good
swimmer, and also basic facts about tigers.

nr   Gardella, Maria Àngels. Un arcón un cofre y un diario.
Illus: Joan Antoni Poch. (Barcelona: La Galera, S. A.,
1981. 125 p.) Gr. 6-10.

In an old, bewitched house a young girl finds an old
diary which contains the stories that Don Pedro Ignacio
Fuentes de Madrigal y Arévalo, Count of Ferrara, used
to tell his niece, María Eugenia. It includes stories
about little angels who ate pens, fairies who lacked vo-
cation, an invasion of "Mercurianos, " a pale Nordic
princess, and the mystery of the bewitched house.
These stories are absurd, wordy, and slow.

nr   Gisbert, Joan Manuel. Escenarios fantásticos. Illus:
Miguel Calatayud. (Barcelona: Editorial Labor, 1979.
191 p.) Gr. 9-12.

The author of these three science fiction stories describes himself as a "journalist who specializes in
themes related to the imaginative and the fantastic. "
Thus these stories tell about his dreams and fantasies.
One story is about an old factory that the author clearly

saw in a dream as a "luminous mansion where all things human acquire a new life. " Another tells about a dance of giant effigies in which the author "cloaked himself in fog. " And the last story takes place in Rainbow Park where the author "could finally talk to the mysterious magician of the imagination. "

These long stories abound in tedious descriptions of senseless dreams and fantasies; the black-and-white illustrations are equally dispirited.

nr _____. El misterio de la isla de Tökland. Illus: Antonio Lenguas. (Madrid: Espasa-Calpe, 1981. 279 p.) Gr. 9-12.

This is a long, vacuous story about a lost island which hides the most "fabulous secret of all times. " Adventurers, scientists and dreamers from all the world are attracted to it in search of treasures and of something marvelous and hideous at the same time. After 273 pages the reader discovers that in our "innermost parts there is a huge Universe comparable to that which is occupied by the sun, the moon, and the stars. . . . But man must banish war and injustice and make all work productive. "

I can't think of any reader who will find this story enjoyable or interesting.

nr Ionescu, Angela C. En el fondo de la caverna. Illus: Néstor Salas. (Barcelona: Editorial Labor, 1980. 134 p.) Gr. 5-7.

This is a collection of six tedious stories with long descriptions and nothing that might incite the interest of young readers. They tell of a man who threw a rock at a cat, of a boy who wanted to learn to play a drum, of children playing with clay, of a man who had been at sea during a storm, of two children who go to the park, and of a girl who saw a scarecrow. The characters are lifeless, the plots are almost nonexistent, and the few black-and-white line illustrations are trite.

m Kurtz, Carmen. Chepita. Illus: Odile. (Madrid: Editorial Escuela Española, 1979. 47 p.) Gr. 4-8.

Chepita was a hump-backed boy who suffered incredible humiliations from his school mates. The boys in school refused to invite him to play with them and went out of their way to embarrass him because of his hump. His mother, whom Chepita adored, had told him that he had two wings on his back: "Dos alitas iguales a las de los angeles. [Two wings similar to the ones angels have.]" Chepita suffered in silence because his mother had also told him, "El bien es más fuerte que el mal ... el bueno tiene la fuerza de mil hombres, porque su corazón es puro. [Good is stronger than evil.... The good person has the strength of a thousand men because his heart is pure.]" p. 39-40. When Chepita saved the life of one of the boys by risking his own, he was accepted by all the boys and was finally invited to play with them.

This is a fast-paced story which certainly holds the reader's interest. The illustrations, however, are too child-like, and the plot is unbelievably cruel.

nr   . Fanfamús. Illus: Odile Kurz. (Barcelona: Editorial Noguer, S. A., 1981. 143 p.) Gr. 8-12.

Fanfamús are all the unborn children. The Fanfamús of this story is a most kind and gentle child/fairy. He assists an old and tired man, he helps old ladies, he helps a mother of many children, he encourages a middle-aged couple to talk to each other, and he helps his paralyzed brother resume a normal life.

This is not an entertaining novel, but rather a strong indictment against abortion. The author insists that "to live is important." "To live is good." "To live is the best thing in the world." "That suffering is also life."

One wonders why Ms. Kurtz chose this medium to express her thoughts about abortion.

m   . Oscar, Buna y el rajá. Illus: Odile Kurz. (Barcelona: Editorial Juventud, 1981. 192 p.) Gr. 7-10.

Oscar and his father won a trip to India. There they meet Sister Mary, a charitable woman who is almost a nun; Sandokán, the director of the great Bazaar in Bombay; Buna, a blind, nineteen-year-old Indian girl;

Ahmad, Buna's adopted father; and other interesting Indian people. Upon arriving in Calcutta, Oscar's father
is involved in an accident which changes their stay in
India from a strictly tourist trip to a long hospital stay
among their newly-found Indian friends.
      Ms. Kurtz's delightful writing style will appeal to
most readers; it is unfortunate, though, that this story
is a little too difficult to read for young readers who
might be interested in Oscar's ingenuous adventures in
India.

nr _____ . Piedras y trompetas. Illus: Odile Kurz.
(Barcelona: Editorial Noguer, 1981. 123 p.) Gr. 4-6.

      These seven stories tell about a good-natured hunter
who lived during the Stone Age; a female giant who had
to give up her manly chores to have a baby; a little
black sheep and her loyal friend, a wolf; a bored princess who decided to learn how to play the trumpet; the
queen of the parrots who confused everything; an enchanted crow who married a beautiful maiden; and a
fairy who always helped others.
      Long descriptions make these stories difficult to read
or enjoy by young children.   Moreover, the black-and-
white illustrations do not add much lightness either.

* _____ . Veva. Illus: Odile Kurz. (Barcelona: Editorial Noguer, S. A. , 1980. 118 p.) Gr. 6-10.

      Veva is a nine-month-old baby girl who can talk and
think like an adult.   She tells about life with her family,
and other amusing experiences that surround her life in
Spain.   She begins by describing her birth, which "[was
something exclusively between my mother and me ... difficult, yes, but if others have done it ... why couldn't
I?]"; her first meal at her mother's breast; her wishes
to be loved by her family; her special relationship with
a gentle and understanding grandmother; and her impa-
tience with her eighteen-year-old sister, Natacha.
      Veva's family is real and thus charms us with all
the jealousy, pain, and joy that occur in a normal, busy
family.   The witty dialogue and humorous situations will
appeal to young readers who will enjoy reading about the
life of a middle-class family in Spain.

*   . Veva y el mar. Illus: Odile Kurz. (Barcelona: Editorial Noguer, 1981. 151 p.) Gr. 7-12.

Veva, a nine-month-old girl, is a charming, intelligent person who can talk and understand like an adult.
In this story she relates her summer experiences with
her delightful grandmother in the Costa Brava. They go
to the beach, visit friends, walk through the nearby
orchards, and, most of all, enjoy the company of Tito,
a long-forgotten relative, who returns from Venezuela
and surprises Grandmother with news of a fabulous in-
heritance.
The simple, natural writing style of this author, as
well as the warmth of a closely-knit Spanish family,
make this story entertaining reading.

nr   Laiglesia, Juan Antonio de. Aventuras de Luciano, farol
     metropolitano. Illus: Juan Fernando D'arrac. (Valla-
     dolid: Miñón, S. A., 1981. 103 p.) Gr. 7-9.

Luciano, a street lantern, relates his life as a re-
sponsible street light. At the beginning, his life was
dull and uninteresting until city people decided to make
drastic changes in the city. They started to use him as
a garbage holder, as a post, and as a display board.
One day he walked away and went to visit the "lantern"
of his dreams. He was caught and returned to his post.
Later on he escapes to the forest where he must explain
himself to the animals and trees of the forest. Finally,
he returns to look for his sweetheart, who had been
transferred to a poor neighborhood. They got married
and live happily ever after.
This is an incredibly lethargic story with inane characters and an absurd plot.

nr   Lanuza, Empar de. El sabio rey loco y otros cuentos.
     Illus: Montserrat Ginesta. (Barcelona: La Galera,
     1979. 120 p.) Gr. 2-4.

These sixteen stories are impossible for young children to read and too childish for older children. They
tell of a wise king who pretended that he was going mad;
of a pencil that enjoyed his work; of a little boy who
learned not to shoot at sparrows; of a boy and his friend,
the chocolate warrior; of a little boy who learned how to

be brave; of another little boy who wanted to be a dog; and other stories.

The long tedious descriptions and complex vocabulary of these stories will certainly not appeal to children.

m   Martín Gaite, Carmen. El castillo de las tres murallas. Illus: Juan Carlos Eguillor. (Barcelona: Editorial Lumen, 1981. 84 p.) Gr. 9-12.

Lucandro, the wealthiest man in the region, lived in a big castle surrounded by three walls. He did not have any friends and did not trust any of his servants. He lived in constant fear of thieves. His beautiful wife, Serena, had to accept a life of total isolation. When Serena gave birth to a lovely girl, Altalé, Lucandro treated the baby as a precious jewel and would not let her mother get near her. Finally Serena elopes with Altalé's music instructor, and Lucandro is devastated by her departure. Altalé grows up as a beautiful and courageous girl who does not fear her father. She, too, elopes with a brave and handsome young man, and Lucandro commits suicide.

Well-drawn characters maintain the reader's interest in this romantic story in a strange setting.

m   Mateos Martín, Pilar. Historias de ninguno. Illus: Juan Antonio Rojo. (Madrid: Ediciones S. M. , 1981. 117 p.) Gr. 4-6.

"Ninguno" is a tiny red-haired boy who is smaller than a marble. In this collection of nine stories the author relates "Ninguno's" amazing experiences at school, at home, and with his friends. He is so tiny that the teacher can barely see him, and thus he must shout to be seen. He also can be of great help when his friends are in trouble as in the case of Rocafu's adventures. Some of these stories are too lengthy and have exaggerated, unbelievable plots; however, the simple writing style of this author and the amusing black-and-white illustrations might appeal to some young readers.

m   Matute, Ana María. El país de la pizarra. Illus: Arturo Heras. (Barcelona: Editorial Lumen, 1978. 32 p.) Gr. 3-5.

This is a fantasy story about a princess who disappeared after a mysterious arithmetic lesson. Long, complicated text detracts from this story with beautiful--although small--illustrations. Older children might be able to comprehend it, but younger children will be confused with the many characters--a young king; the princess; a teacher; a magic star; a fairy ladybird; a carpenter; and the four young children who finally assist the princess in solving the addition problem, thus helping her return to her palace.

*   Molina Llorente, Pilar. El mensaje de maese Zamaor.
     Illus: Francisco Sole. (Madrid: Ediciones S. M. , 1981.
     107 p.) Gr. 6-10.

     Maese Zamaor, court painter of Cártulo II, is selected by the King for a dangerous mission: He must deliver a secret document to the king's cousin, the Prince of Zarduña, if the kingdom is to survive. Maese Zamaor experiences many hardships and humiliations as he confronts abusive landlords, thieves, and traitors, as well as suffering hunger, cold, and lack of sleep. By using his talents as an artist, his intelligence, and his courage, Zamaor discovers the traitor and saves the kingdom of Cártulo II, King of Fartuel.
     The adventures and excitement of Maese Zamaor's difficult journey are an engrossing story which will maintain the interest of young readers. Eight black-and-white line illustrations excellently depict the life of a brave Spanish artist and courier.

m   Muñoz Martín, Juan. Fray Perico y su borrico. Illus:
     Antonio Tello. (Madrid: Ediciones S. M. , 1980. 142
     p.) Gr. 6-8.

     Twenty serious friars lived in an old convent close to Salamanca. They prayed, studied, and worked together every day. There was a studious friar and an architect friar, as well as a dumb friar. The peaceful life at the convent ended when Fray Perico was admitted as an apprentice. He couldn't read, or write, or do arithmetic, and he seemed to be constantly getting in trouble. He adopted an old donkey, and this didn't make matters any better. After the donkey he took in a wolf, three goats, and five pigs. Fray Perico, who always meant well and was eager to help all sick and needy souls, finally won the support and friendship of all the friars at the convent.

Fray Perico is a charming character, but most young readers from the 6th to the 8th grade will find the adventures too childish. Unfortunately, the vocabulary and sentence construction are too difficult for younger readers, who might enjoy reading about "Fray Perico y su borrico" (Fray Perico and his donkey).

nr   Ortiz, Lourdes.   La caja de lo que pudo ser.   Illus: Montse Ginesta.   (Madrid: Ediciones Altea, 1981.   29 p.)   Gr. 6-9.

Jaime was given a little box that could change the course of history.   If he pressed it, he could avoid murders that led to wars, Columbus' discovery of America, and the Third World War.   Jaime loved to read history books and, with his little box, challenged the teacher's explanations of historical facts.

This is a most absurd and complicated story that is neither entertaining nor enlightening.

*   Osorio, Marta.   El último elefante blanco.   Illus: Maite Miralles.   (Valladolid: Editorial Miñón, 1980.   56 p.) Gr. 6-8.

This book contains two fast-moving stories about animals in the Orient--India and Tibet--that include suspense and adventure.   "El último elefante blanco" tells about Kamala, a white elephant that grew up in captivity, and Raktamukha, a vagabond monkey.   They became good friends and together found a way to free Kamala, take him back to the forest where he was born, and allow him to live a normal life with other grey elephants. "El aguilucho" is about Nan Singh, a kind-hearted monk and Kang Rimpoche, a young eagle.   Nan Singh saved Kang Rimpoche from two hunters that were going to kill her and cared for her during her early years.   When they had to part, they still remained close and helped each other whenever they were in danger.

These well-written stories will entertain young readers with their exciting plots and adorable characters. The black-and-white illustrations convey very well Indian and Tibetan moods.

nr Pacheco, M. A., and J. L. García Sánchez. Soy un
    niño. Illus: Asun Balzola. (Madrid: Ediciones Altea,
    1974. 32 p.) Gr. 4-8.

This is indeed a confusing book about a fat boy who
tells his story about love and life. It begins by stating
that originally he lived inside his mother for nine months
--appropriate illustrations show how he grew inside his
mother's body--and then highlights important episodes in
his early years, such as nursing at his mother's breast.
When he was older he discovered that children are born
after a male and a female love each other, but he never
learned how not to feel lonely. Finally, he met a skinny
girl and, because they both felt very lonely, they decided
to have children. They waited nine months in which
time they became very good friends; however, they did
not have children because: "Lo único que pueden hacer
los niños es crecer ... y jugar ... y aprender. [The
only thing that children can do is grow ... and play ...
and learn.]" Modern, watercolor illustrations show children at play and learning about "love." This book is
certain to arouse strong emotions in many adults and to
confuse young readers because of its bewildering message.

m   Puncel, María Abuelita Opalina. Illus: Margarita Pun-
    cel. (Madrid: Ediciones SM, 1981. 86 p.) Gr. 4-6.

Isa has to write a brief story about her grandmother.
But Isa has a problem--she doesn't have a grandmother.
So the teacher tells her to invent her favorite grandmother. By borrowing from all her friends' grandmothers, Isa writes about her "Abuelita Opalina." Her friends
object, and Isa is pleasantly surprised when her father
brings home his aunt, whom she may call "Grandmother
Nieves."
The illustrations, characters, and plot are appropriate for children in grades second through fourth; but, unfortunately, this story includes too much text and lengthy
descriptions for them to be able to understand it.

*   _____. Cuando sea mayor haré cine. Illus: Arcadio
    Lobato. (Madrid: Ediciones Altea, 1979. 45 p.) Gr.
    5-8.

A young girl relates her experiences in a movie

studio. Her mother needed a make-up assistant, and
thus the reader learns about various people who are involved in making movies, such as the director, producer,
photographer, actors, actresses, and others. It emphasizes the hard work of film making and the importance
of good planning. Amusing illustrations complement the
witty and informative text.

*   . Cuando sea mayor seré comerciante. Illus:
María Rius. (Madrid: Ediciones Altea, 1979. 45 p.)
Gr. 5-8.

Through the eyes of Ana and Manuel, young readers
are exposed to the life of small business people. It includes examples of various types of businesses (e. g. , a
bakery, pharmacy, grocery store, flower shop) and the
problems associated with running a successful store. It
emphasizes that it is not easy to make money operating
a business. This is a well-conceived introduction to the
world of retailing with attractive, colorful illustrations
on every page.

*   . Cuando sea mayor seré enfermera. Illus:
Ulises Wensell. (Madrid: Ediciones Altea, 1979. 45
p.) Gr. 5-8.

A young girl falls from her bicycle and is taken to
the emergency ward at the hospital. There she learns
about the importance of nurses in caring for sick people.
Nurses are shown taking X-rays, assisting in surgery,
feeding patients, making beds, analyzing blood, giving
information, and many other activities. The informative
text is complemented by interesting illustrations. Perhaps one should object to the sexual stereotypes: All
the doctors in the story are males; all the nurses are
females.

*   . Cuando sea mayor seré marino. Illus:
Ulises Wensel. (Madrid: Ediciones Altea, 1979. 45
p.) Gr. 5-8.

Through the eyes of an approximately twelve-year-
old boy, young readers are exposed to the life of a sea-
man. It describes many duties that must be performed

to keep a boat in good condition, as well as the comforts
and problems of life at sea.   It emphasizes the education
and preparation necessary to become an expert and the
various types of boats that are available.   There is action and excitement in this introduction to seafaring.
Colorful illustrations complement each page.

*   .   Cuando sea mayor trabajaré en una granja.
Illus: Letizia Galli.   (Madrid: Ediciones Altea, 1979.
45 p.) Gr. 5-8.

    Despite her protests, a young girl from the city is
sent to live with her aunt and uncle on a farm.   Gradually, she is exposed to many activities that are constantly
taking place on a farm: milking cows, shearing sheep,
harvesting vegetables and fruits, classifying eggs, and
others.   She also learns that there are many other duties
related to operating a successful farm, such as keeping
records and preparing invoices of products sold.   Colorful illustrations of life on a farm complement the simple
and informative text.

m   .   El hombre de la lluvia.   (Madrid: Ediciones
Altea, 1981.   29 p.)   Gr. 4-6.

    An old man who takes care of a lighthouse is going
to be replaced by an electric light.   He feels sad and
useless.   Suddenly one night, he heard a little cloud that
was stuck on a lightning rod.   He freed the little cloud,
and thus they become good friends.   They traveled together and gave water to whoever needed it.   The old
man became happy again.
    The simple, watercolor illustrations make this book
appropriate for young children, but the text is too long
and perplexing for young children to understand.

nr Robles, Antonio.   La bruja Doña Paz.   Illus: Asun Balzola.   (Valladolid: Miñón, 1981.   68 p.)   Gr. 6-8.

    This is not a story for young readers, but rather a
wearisome sermon about the evilness of war, the joy of
peace, and the beauty of love and brotherhood among
men.   The author uses the main character, a kind and
gentle witch called Doña Paz (Doña Peace), to endlessly

repeat his message to all the children--white, black, and yellow--of the world: "Live peacefully. " "Do not hate. " "Long live peace. "

I certainly hope that no child will be forced to read this uninspired and dense discourse.

nr   Roig Castellanos, Mercedes.   Piripitusa.   Illus: Asun Balzola.   (Barcelona: Editorial Noguer, 1981.   109 p.) Gr. 5-8.

Piripitusa, a young female dragon, suddenly lost her parents.   She was sad and lonely when, to her surprise, the animals of the forest offered her their friendship in exchange for her protection.   The forest lost its peacefulness when a witch and other thieves tried to steal a young princess's treasure.   Thanks to Piripitusa and her forest friends the treasure was saved and peace returned to their forest.

This is a long, slow-moving fantasy story which is too wordy for older children and too confusing for young children.   The black-and-white line illustrations are equally lethargic.

nr   Sennell, Joles.   La guía fantástica.   Illus: Horacio Elena.   (Madrid: Editorial Juventud, 1979.   127 p.) Gr. 8-10.

This is a series of fantasy stories about unicorns which can only be seen by people who have good imaginations.   These people can do amazing work or go to incredible places.   The second part of this book tells about a fantastic book which could only be read by certain people at certain times--otherwise its pages were blank and the book had to be given to another reader. A few black-and-white illustrations complement the listless text.

*   Sierra I. Fabra, Jordi.   El cazador.   (Madrid: Ediciones S. M. , 1981.   213 p.)   Gr. 10-adult.

Dubal is a fifty-seven-year-old trapper who had never killed an animal in his life.   He starts feeling old and decides to go into the forest for the last time to trap a live tiger without using any weapons.   During the

trip he remembers brief episodes of his life and wonders
what he is truly after. Suddenly, he finds his victims--
a tiger and a tigress. He intends to capture the tigress
without killing the tiger and return to his town. There
is much excitement in the trapper's efforts to return
safely and in the tiger's efforts to save his beloved tigress. Dubal's genuine doubts and apprehensions about
his own future and his extraordinary efforts to save his
own life without killing the furious tiger are marvelously
depicted.

Young adults will be fascinated by this fast-moving
story of an aging hunter in search of his own future as
well as his appreciation of life and love. Some readers
might find the love scenes between Dubal and his wife
and the tiger and tigress a little too explicit; but, they
are definitely an integral part of this novel which, as
the author states in the prologue, "is the story of a tiger's love. "

nr Valls, Alvar. El mensaje del caballero del Aguila Ram-
pante. Illus: Ricard Castells. (Barcelona: La Galera,
1979. 111 p.) Gr. 6-8.

A good-natured gang of three girls and five boys
finds a mysterious message written in the thirteenth
century. They decide to investigate and after overcoming "incredible" difficulties they encounter fantastic treasures which consist of beautiful paintings and armors of
the Middle Ages. As they try to leave through a long,
dark and narrow tunnel, they notice they are trapped and
can't get out. Suddenly, they are saved by kind and
loyal friends. The whole town honors the "heroes and
heroines" because of their great historical and artistic
discovery.

This is a simplistic, childish story which will not
interest young readers.

*   Vallverdú, Josep. El alcalde chatarra. Illus: Josep
Gual. (Barcelona: La Galera, 1981. 141 p.) Gr. 8-
12.

Chatarra, a lonely and courageous man, decides to
stay in his town despite the proximity of the enemy's
army. He proclaims himself mayor, and thus he re-
solves to save his town from plunder and destruction.

Jana, a young girl, and a group of abandoned teenagers,
as well as Chatarra, the newly proclaimed mayor, demonstrate their loyalty and valor as well as their respect and
affection for each other which ultimately save the town.

There is much action in this warm-hearted story of
a man who overcomes his own loneliness and, in so doing,
finds his own happiness.

m _____. Los amigos del viento. Illus: Pilarín Bayés.
(Barcelona: La Galera, 1979. 127 p.) Gr. 8-10.

This novel takes place in Spain during the time of
Napoleon's invasion of the Iberian Peninsula between 1808
and 1809. Miguel Vernet, a Spanish patriot, must escape from the French, who recently occupied his home-
town in Catalunia. His two children, Quel and Antonia,
remain behind and an order is issued for their arrest.
Odila, a brave and intelligent neighbor, plans a most
original escape in which the children fly over the French
forces and safely meet their father aboard an English
ship. Unfortunately, this story is written for older children, who will find some of the adventures and illustrations too childish. Younger children might enjoy the
story, but they will find the vocabulary and sentence
structure too difficult to read and/or understand.

m _____. Aventura en la azotea. Illus: Joan Gomez.
(Barcelona: La Galera, S. A., 1981. 55 p.) Gr. 5-7.

Agustín was elected the best liked student in his
class. As a prize he received a silent duck. On his
way home from school, the duck escaped into the roofs
of some tall buildings. There he was greeted by a thief
who wanted to use Agustín as a hostage. Unexpectedly,
Merengue, the duck, scared the thief who was quickly
overpowered by a police officer. Agustín was allowed
to take a taxi home and show Merengue to his mother.

Some young readers might enjoy Agustín's adventures
with his silent duck, even though the illustrations depict
a young boy, approximately eight years old, who seems
inordinately devoted to his duck.

* _____. Cita en la cala negra. Illus: Arcadio Lo-
bato. (Barcelona: Editorial Noguer, 1981. 133 p.)
Gr. 7-10.

Tomás and Patrick, two teenage boys, are spending
their holidays in a resort close to Barcelona. Unexpectedly, they get involved in an exciting mystery where
they save Llonch, a wounded man, and later assist the
Spanish police in locating a group of thieves, as well as
the stolen jewels. Tomás is questioned by his father
about the strange happenings and is forced to report the
incidents to the police. In the meantime, Patrick is
kidnapped and beaten by one of the thieves. Patrick's
and Llonch's escape from their captors seems a little too
easy; nevertheless, this is a fast-paced mystery story
which will surely interest young readers. Black-and-
white, line illustrations add animation to the story.

nr _____. Girasol de historias. Illus: Frederic An-
guera. (Barcelona: La Galera, S. A., 1980. 125 p.)
Gr. 8-10.

The author's purpose in writing this collection of
ten short stories is to describe the reality in which we
live, to portray different ways of life that exist in this
world, and to convey to young readers his "positive in-
tentions"--namely, his interest in conservation, his op-
position to violence and oppression, and his respect for
human beings. Each story is set in a different area of
the world including the Andes, Japan, Indochina, the
Middle East, and others. The result is a collection of
bland stories which lack interest. The climax of most
of the stories is the author's message to his readers.
For example, the following is the ending of "El Barrio
de la Calabaza": "Y los vecinos del Barrio de la Calabaza tuvieron la impresión de que, al final, aquella aventura de las calabazas gigantes había servido para pro-
porcionar alegría a la gente. Siempre que hagáis algo,
que sirva para que alguién sonría y goce unos momentos
de felicidad. Tenedlo en cuenta. [And the neighbors of
the Barrio de la Calabaza had the impression that, at
the end, the adventure of the giant pumpkins had served
to give happiness to the people. Whenever you do something that makes someone smile and enjoy a few moments
of happiness, keep it in mind.]" (p. 89).

nr _____. Las vacaciones del reloj. Illus: Joan Antoni Poch. (Barcelona: La Galera, S. A., 1981. 54 p.)
Gr. 5-8.

A family of four--mother, father, brother, and sister--get ready to go on a week's vacation. They close up the house, and the only object that continues to work is the big old clock--it never gets a vacation. Some of the objects in the house decide to have a good time while the owners of the house are on vacation. Two porcelain figurines dance and flirt with each other, and a rag doll goes through all the closets and drawers in the house. When the family returns, the old clock decides that it, too, deserves a vacation and stops working for eight days.

Fifth through eighth graders will not find this fantasy story interesting or appealing.

nr   Vannini, Marisa. _La fogata._ (Barcelona: Editorial Juventud, S. A., 1979. 240 p.) Gr. 9-12.

Pantolín, a thirteen-year-old boy from Venezuela, is desperate to find out about his parents. He was abandoned when he was one year old, and since then he has lived with three men--a farmer, a musician, and a landholder. In his disconsolate search for his own background, he goes on a long trip where he lives with three different ethnic groups. From the Waika Indians, who live in a forest between Venezuela and Brazil, he learns that it is "fantastic not to possess material wealth--they had life, feelings, spirit and the forest." He also learned that they incinerate their dead ones, suffer hunger, and lack schools. Then he lives among Jewish people, where he learns about the persecutions and sufferings of the Jews around the world, especially during World War II. His third stop is a village in the mountains of Venezuela where many people from Sardinia (Italy) live. There he realizes that "everyone was a friend and everyone was human, because he had seen their joys and worries, their pains and successes, their doubts and their courage." So after returning home to his three "fathers," he is committed to helping others: "pensar en los demás es ser uno mismo; [to think of others is to be oneself]" p. 233.

I doubt that young adults will enjoy this book. It is not a novel, as the plot and characters are only sociological symbols for the author's messages about friendship, humanity, peace, and so forth.

m   Vázquez-Vigo, Carmen. <u>Animales charlatanes.</u> Illus:
María Dolores de León. (Barcelona: Editorial Noguer,
S. A., 1980. 107 p.) Gr. 3-5.

These are the stories of seven chattering animals
that tell about their special personalities: a cat that
reads the dictionary, a duckbill platypus that is confused
about its personality, a hippopotamus that doesn't want
to be called fat, a pigeon that spends its life in strange
places, a donkey that wishes to be free, a sad serpent,
and an owl with lovely eyes.
Young children would really enjoy these stories if
they were written in a much simpler language. Also,
young children need more illustrations than the few which
are included in this book.

*   . <u>Caramelos de menta.</u> Illus: Antonio Tello.
(Madrid: S. M. Ediciones, 1981. 132 p.) Gr. 6-8.

Four boys and one girl must come up with money to
pay for damages to the owner of a chicken and egg store,
which were caused by their newly-found dog, Dragon.
They try everything they can think of--selling candy, de-
livering baked goods, playing football, entering dog con-
tests--but they don't have enough money. Surprisingly,
Dragon finds his previous owner, who is delighted to give
them the money to pay for the damages, as well as to
get the boys the things they most wanted: a skeleton,
a soccer ball, and cakes.
The unaffected style of this author, as well as the
entertaining dialogue, make this story a refreshing encounter with Spanish young people.

m   . <u>Guau.</u> Illus: Asun Balzola. (Barcelona:
Editorial Noguer, 1980. 109 p.) Gr. 5-8.

These are four stories in which all the principal
characters are dogs. Ugly dog is sad because he cannot
find a home. Finally, his friend rat helps him find a
kind master who takes him to his home. The artist dog
works in the movies and can't understand why another
dog would not want to join him as an actor. Ferocious
dog is truly a friendly dog who only looks fierce. And
freedom-loving dog refuses to help his master hunt--
he is a dog who has principles.

These stories might appeal to dog lovers, as they are written in an easy-to-understand manner. It includes a few black-and-white line drawings of various types of dogs.

*   _____. El rey que voló. Illus: Karin Schubert. (Madrid: Ediciones Altea, 1980. 29 p.) Gr. 3-6.

This is a delightful story about a wicked king who burdened his court with his incessant demands. On the one thousandth anniversary of the foundation of his kingdom, he decided to have an elaborate celebration. He ordered a new dancing hall, extravagant parades, and the most majestic long, wide gown ever made. The court tailor panicked, as he knew how difficult to please the king was. However, his courageous friend, Alicia, helped him, and the gown was finished on time. The king's reactions to the gown and a mysterious prank played by another tailor keep this story exciting until the end when Alicia and her friends get rid of the ungrateful king. Amusing, colorful illustrations complement the easy-to-read text.

HISTORICAL FICTION

nr   Amo, Montserrat del. La piedra y el agua. Illus: Juan-Ramón Alonso Díaz-Toledano. (Barcelona: Editorial Noguer, S. A. , 1981. 197 p.) Gr. 9-12.

The stories of Dusco, the conqueror of fire, and Titul, the architect who brought water to the tribe, are told in a lethargic and presumptuous manner. In addition it includes the adventures of Dusco against a mammoth (a primitive elephant that is now extinct) and Dusco against a bear; but the book's message is that "man wished to use fire so that all men could overcome together hunger and thirst, cold and drought, fear and violence, in service of man. " Inert, black-and-white illustrations of primitive people are as bad as the story.

*   Barceló I. Cullerés, Joan. Ojos de jineta. Illus: Jordi Bulbena. (Barcelona: La Galera, 1979. 125 p.) Gr. 9-12.

By combining magic, witchcraft, astrology, alchemy, and the inquisition in sixteenth century Spain, the author wrote a fast-moving story which relates the abuses and tortures against the Jews in Spain. Eloim, a young Jewish boy, and his magician friend, Banga, resort to magical powers to save Eloim's father, Jonas, who had been imprisoned and tortured by the corrupt judges of the Inquisition. There is much fantasy in this novel which may not appeal to some readers. Others will be enthralled with the adventure and suspense as well as with Eloim's fantastic victory, thanks to his "invincible" friends. Powerful black-and-white illustrations perfectly depict life in Spain during this dark era.

*   Cabré, Jaume. El extraño viaje que nadie se creyó (La historia que Roc Pons no conocía). Illus: Joan Andreu Vallvé. (Barcelona: La Galera, 1980. 118 p.) Gr. 6-10.

Roc Pons, a fourteen-year-old boy from Barcelona, found himself in a strange century. He left his house one summer afternoon in 1980, and suddenly realized he was in Barcelona in 1714--the year the city was blockaded by Castilian and French armies which supported Phillip V. Black-and-white line illustrations and a fast-paced text convey to readers the feelings of the people of Barcelona that preceded the surrender of their city. Roc's adventures and dilemmas add much interest and excitement to this story, which was written by the author as a homage to his city, Barcelona, in its fight for freedom.

*   Vallverdú, Josep. Mir el "ardilla. " Illus: Joan Andreu Vallvé. (Barcelona: La Galera, 1978. 120 p.) Gr. 7-10.

Life in the eleventh century in Spain is excellently portrayed in this fast-paced story about Moors and Christians. Mir, a brave young boy, and Llop, his father, are repeatedly involved in saving the lives of many Christians as they settle lands which used to belong to the Arabs. Amidst war, adventure, and excitement Mir and Llop emerge as courageous and honest warriors who triumph against a cruel and treacherous Moorish leader. The misunderstandings between Moors and Christians during this era are also very well explained. The well-

drawn characterizations of Mir and Llop make this novel
delightful reading.   Sensitive black-and-white illustrations
add much interest to this historical novel of Spain during
the Reconquest Period.

NONFICTION

m   Balzola, Asun.   Los colores.   (Madrid: Ediciones Encuentro, 1980?   14 p.)   Gr. 1-3.

   Six colors--red, blue, yellow, green, gray, and
white--are introduced to children through common objects:
an apple, Little Red Riding Hood, the sky, the ocean,
the sun, flowers, grass, trees, and snow.   Unfortunately,
the lifeless illustrations detract from the book's potential
interest.

m   . Los números.   (Madrid: Ediciones Encuentro,
1980?   21 p.)   Gr. 1-3.

   The numbers "one" to "ten" are introduced to children through a simple text.   Unfortunately, the blurred
illustrations in watercolor are too bland or confusing to
appeal to young readers.

POETRY

*   Bravo-Villasante, Carmen.   Adivina adivinanza.   Folklore infantil.   (Madrid: Interduc/Schroedel, 1978.
80 p.)   Gr. K-5.

   This is an amusing collection of traditional riddles,
tongue-twisters, singing games, nursery rhymes, Christmas carols, and prayers that are well known in Spanish-
speaking countries.   The brevity and sense of word play
inherent in the Hispanic oral tradition are beautifully
maintained for children.   The illustrations are nineteenth-
century lithographs in color; some are quite charming;
others are a little too cute.

*   . China, China, Capuchina, en esta mano está
la china.   Illus: Carmen Andrada.   (Valladolid: Miñón,
1981.   106 p.)   Gr. PK-4.

This is a delightful collection of traditional Hispanic children's rhymes, riddles, games, and songs. Unfortunately, the black-and-white, undersized illustrations do not add much excitement to these rhymes and games which, as this well-known author states, are "alegría y poesía [happiness and poetry]." Nevertheless, there is a wealth of joy in their simplicity and charm so that young children will enjoy reading or being read to.

nr   Ferrán, Jaime. La playa larga. Illus: Adolfo Calleja. (Valladolid: Editorial Miñón, 1981. 49 p.) Gr. 8-12.

Melodramatically, the author reminisces about his visits to the long beach. In a poetic manner, he tells how nothing has changed at the beach since his childhood; yet, he later describes his efforts at cleaning up all the trash that people who don't love the beach have left behind. The author also philosophizes about the sea:

"El mar es una cuna
en la que cabe todo
El mar es una tumba
donde nadie está solo.
Del mar vino la vida
hasta dar con nosotros.
Al mar regresaremos
un día u otro" (p. 36)

Very few readers will be interested in this author's feelings about "his beach." Abstract, black-and-white line illustrations complement the poetic text.

RELIGIOUS BOOKS

m   Perez-Lucas, Ma. Dolores. Teresa de Jesús cuenta su vida a los niños de hoy. (Alcoy: Editorial Marfil, S. A. , 1981. 64 p.) Gr. 6-10.

The miraculous and exemplary religious life of Teresa de Jesús is narrated in a fast-moving text. It tells about her parents, brothers, and sisters and her desires to enter a convent despite her father's objections. There are many examples of Teresa de Jesús' religious zeal as well as her dedication in founding new convents. It should be noted that this story upholds strong Catholic sentiments regarding other religious groups or people. For example, "Tal vez nos habían raptado los judíos o los moros. No sería el primer caso que se daba. " [Perhaps we would have been kidnapped by the Jews or Moors. It wouldn't have been the first time.]   (p. 16). Appropriate black-and-white, watercolor illustrations complement the text.

nr   Salvador, Tomás.   San Pedro portero del cielo.   Illus: Carlos Torres.   (Madrid: Ediciones 29, 1979.   56 p.) Gr. 8-12.

The Lord made Peter the major gate-keeper of the Kingdom of Heaven.   He instructed him to be just and to open the door to all the humble and clean of heart.   This story relates Peter's dilemmas in admitting to heaven a man who wouldn't depart from his donkey, a simple man who couldn't make up his mind whether to go in or stay out, a mailman who lost a letter, an astronaut who was lost in space, an old woman who drank too much, a student who always failed in school, a general who never won a battle, an author who wrote the most beautiful story, and other difficult cases.

The constant emphasis on "good" people with infinite patience, faith, and pity who are certainly welcome in heaven, does not make for enjoyable reading.   The illustrations are neither inspiring nor appealing.

THEATER

nr   Armijo, Consuelo.   Bam, Bim, Bom, ¡Arriba el telón! Illus: Carmen Andrada.   (Valladolid: Editorial Miñón, 1981.   105 p.)   Gr. 5-7.

Six plays that the author believes can be "represented, seen, and read by children. "   Unfortunately, though, the long, complicated dialogues are too difficult for younger children to understand, and the themes of the plays are too childish for older children.   They tell of a king who wished to have one birthday party in the summer and one in the winter, of drawfs and a giant who exchanged boots and caps, of two old men who constantly argue about birds in winter and other absurd, uninteresting themes. The black-and-white line illustrations are senseless as well as insipid.

m   Fuertes, Gloria. Las tres reinas magas. Illus: Ulises
    Wensell. (Madrid: Editorial Escuela Española, 1979.
    45 p.) Gr. 5-7.

        Witty play about the Three Wise Queens--Melchora,
    Gaspara, and Baltasara--who are on their way to visit
    the Newborn Child. The first part of the play is espe-
    cially amusing, as the three queens decide to enjoy them-
    selves by drinking anís (a Spanish liqueur) and by com-
    plaining about the discomforts of the trip. The following
    is an example of the buoyancy of the language:

        "Gaspara:
            ¡Madre del amor hermoso,
            que viaje tan horroroso! ...
            Lo que faltaba para el duro
            -con este tiempo tan crudo" (p. 15)

    Unfortunately, in the second act the jollity is exchanged
    for a diatribe against war and the play ends by the three
    queens singing:

            "¡Qué podemos dejar,
            a todos los niños del mundo,
            un 'juguete' de Paz!

            [What can we leave
            to all the children of the world,
            a 'toy' of Peace!]" (p. 38)

        The jocose, colorful illustrations add a beautiful
    tone to the play.

nr Vázquez-Vigo, Carmen. Aire de colores. Illus: Viví
    Escrivá. (Valladolid: Miñón, S. A., 1981? 88 p.) Gr.
    5-7.

        The purpose of this play for children is to teach
    young readers/listeners that "a day without laughter is
    a lost day. That this is a day to learn to give your
    hand to a friend, to be happy. " Hence, seven characters
    endlessly dialogue about the seven wonders of the world,
    a hidden treasure, the importance of asking questions,
    and other "significant" concepts. The only redeeming
    quality of this book is the black-and-white illustrations
    which should appeal to younger children.

FICTION

nr Baudisch, Iris de. Chicho. (Montevideo: Editorial Goes,
1979. 16 p.) Gr. 7-9.

    This melodramatic story is about an ownerless dog
that was "all love, kindness, and fidelity. " He was ignored by everyone until he found a "good, lonely, and
silent girl" who never knew that his name was "simply
Chicho" and who had only one feeling for him: "LOVE. "
    There are too many imposing concepts in this vacu-
ous story: kindness, love, generosity, goodness, and
so forth.

m Davila Castro, Pablo Christian. Mi amiga Capi. Illus:
William Gezzio. (Montevideo: Acali Editorial, 1980.
12 p.) Gr. 4-6.

    A young boy went with his father to the forest.
There he found a baby beaver which he promised to take
care of himself. They became good friends and did
everything together. Suddenly, one day his father explained that Capi, the beaver, did not need him any longer
and had to go back to the forest. Despite his sadness,
the young boy understood that when you love someone you
want him to be happy.
    This is a touching story about a boy's relationship
with his pet. Unfortunately, the two-tone illustrations
are bland and ordinary.

nr Firpo, José María. Los indios eran muy penetrantes.
(Montevideo: Arca Editorial, 1981. 94 p.) Gr. 6-8.

This is a collection of twenty-six brief essays and
dialogues about slavery, brushing one's teeth, digestion,
weather, fish, spiders, Indians, summer holidays, and
other unrelated subjects. Perhaps the brevity of these
essays--a series of one-sentence statements--might appeal to some readers. However, they lack a basic theme
or structure.

m   . La sólida e inesperada muerte de Solís.
(Montevideo: Arca Editorial, 1981. 92 p.) Gr. 7-10.

In homage to her husband, Mrs. Firpo collected
these definitions and dialogues written by José María
Firpo's students. It includes a series of one-sentence
statements on various topics such as gold, "if I had $100, "
a substitute teacher, "did you know?, " a visit to Coca-
Cola, and others. The brevity and simplicity of these
dialogues and definitions might amuse some readers.

nr Murguía, Julián. Cuentos para Juan Manuel (Estampas
de pueblo y campo). Illus: William Gezzio. (Montevideo: Acali Editorial, 1980. 20 p.) Gr. 5-8.

Melancholically, the author describes his feelings
about his town: the sadness of the citrus trees, the
beauty of butterflies, the importance of planting corn,
his kind grandfather, the train that came to town, and
other remembrances.
Young readers will be bored by these long, tedious
"personal sketches. "

nr Obaldía, José María. Lejos, allá y ayer. Illus: William
Gezzio. (Montevideo: Acali Editorial, 1980. 21 p.) Gr.
6-9.

These six stories tell about the author's younger
days: winter holidays with a hard-working uncle, carnival time, flying kites, summer holidays, eating biscuits,
and playing with tops.
Neither the two-tone illustrations nor the long, wearisome text will appeal to young readers.

nr Puentes de Oyenard, Sylvia. Con un ojito abierto. Illus:

by children. (Montevideo: Ediciones Geminis, 1979.
40 p.) Gr. 6-8.

This is a collection of nine stories about animals,
magicians, fairies, and pirates, which are too long and
difficult to be read by young children and too childish
for older readers. The two-tone illustrations by children
ages seven through eleven are simple and sweet.

nr Speranza, Rolando. El globo amarillo. Illus: William
Gezzio. (Montevideo: Acali Editorial, 1980. 12 p.)
Gr. 4-6.

Guillermo, a little boy, was the proud owner of the
world's biggest yellow balloon. The balloon was so big
that it pulled Guillermo high up in the sky. Amid his
parents' and friends' consternation, Guillermo kept going
up and up. Suddenly, a seagull pinched the balloon,
caught Guillermo by his clothes, and dropped him at his
house. This story is too childish for older children and
too difficult to read for younger children.

m Tabaré Fernández Salinas, Alfredo. Sobre gatos y
ratones. Illus: William Gezzio. (Montevideo: Acali
Editorial, 1980. 11 p.) Gr. 4-6.

Small and peaceful animals of the forest got together
to discuss the problems of the pumas' constant attacks.
They decided to make a lion's wig to put on a puma, and
a mouse volunteered to put the wig on the sleeping puma's
head. This fooled the puma into believing that he was a
lion. And because male lions don't hunt for food, but
rather wait for female lions to bring it to them, he
starved. Thus, the small animals triumphed over the
pumas. Uninspired two-tone illustrations complement
the amusing text.

nr Valin de Vallespir, Stella Maris. Jesusín el polizón.
(Montevideo: Talleres Gráficos La Paz, 1980. 86 p.)
Gr. 6-10.

These four moralistic stories and seventeen saccharine poems will certainly bore all readers. The long
descriptions, "angelic" characters, and dull messages--

study hard, love thy neighbor, honor your parents, be
good--are not recommended reading for anyone.

nr   Viera, María de los Angeles. En el país de Nipón-Nipo
y la luna de verdad. (Montevideo: Centro de Investi-
gación y Experimentación Pedagógica, 1979. [20 p.])
Gr. 3-5.

Nipón-Nipo was the moon's best friend. So when the
sun asked the moon to hide during the day, the moon
had nowhere to go but to Nipón-Nipo's house. This made
Nipón-Nipo very happy. And since that day, Nipón-Nipo
and the moon have lived happily together. Unappealing,
black-and-white illustrations and a slow-moving text make
this story difficult to enjoy.

POETRY

nr   Andrade de Ramos, Celestina. Pitangas. (Sarandí
Grande: Imprenta Sarandí, 1980. 48 p.) Gr. 5-8.

Included are thirty-two saccharine, overly sentimental poems about animals, spring, my country, my
dreams, and other topics that lack interest. Neither the
uninspired black-and-white illustrations nor the wearisome poems will appeal to young readers.

nr   Figueira, Gastón. Para los niños de América. (Montevideo: Biblioteca Alfar, 1980. 140 p.) Gr. 8-12.

This is a collection of approximately one hundred
poems and ten brief legends that "should serve as moral
and patriotic guides to young readers." Thus there are
poems about the beauty and greatness of life; young, free
butterflies; the justice and nobility of young citizens; the
ennobling power of books; the joy of living; and many others. Even though the author has worthy thoughts indeed,
these poems and legends are dull and insipid.

nr   Guerendiaín Morales, Kitita. Cajón de cachivaches.
Illus: Auria Lafitte. (Montevideo: Impresora Record,
1979. 50 p.) Gr. 3-6.

This is a collection of twenty-five saccharine poems about animals, toys, and other things common to young children. Neither the eight uninspired black-and-white illustrations nor the overly sweet poems will appeal to children.

FICTION

m Almeida, Fernanda Lopes de, and Alcy Linares. La
curiosidad premiada. (Caracas: Ediciones Ekaré-Banco
del Libro, 1979. 32 p.) Gr. 3-5.

Mariana was a very curious little girl--she asked
questions all the time. Her parents and teacher were
desperate, and finally her parents went to Doña Benita,
an old--but young--teacher, for advice. Doña Benita
concluded that Mariana suffered from accumulated curiosity and recommended that her parents start answering
all her questions. So Mariana continued to ask, and her
parents also decided to start asking questions. The family asked the astronomer at the observatory about the
sky and the stars. They also went to the zoo and asked
about trees and animals. Mariana's parents were delighted with their daughter's curiosity, which showed
them that they lived in a most interesting world.
One wonders if this story is meant for children or
their parents. The simple text and amusing illustrations
might appeal to children. But a little girl asking questions all the time does not make for an entertaining
story, except as a lesson to parents.

nr Alvarez de Vernet, Ana Mercedes. Cuentos venezolanos.
(Caracas: Cultural Venezolana, 1978. 103 p.) Gr. 6-8.

This is a collection of fourteen stories that are full
of good examples for young readers. Some teach them
to have confidence in themselves, others encourage them
to love their country--Venezuela--so that they may make
it one of the greatest countries in the world; others in-

spire them to be kind and charitable towards their friends; and others inform them about the benefits of being good and studious.

Neither the spiritless illustrations nor the virtuous text will inspire young readers to enjoy these stories.

nr   Araujo, Orlando. El niño que llegó hasta el sol. Illus: Alejandro Otero. (Caracas: Ediciones María di Mase, 1979. 27 p.) Gr. 8-10.

Perhaps the message of this book is to show how a person becomes a painter, sculptor, and architect--otherwise, it is difficult to understand. It includes striking modernistic paintings and photographs which do not always correspond to the text. The narration tells of a very poor family; suddenly, the father dies, and there are several pages that describe the son's feelings about his father's death. Suddenly again, the boy is taken to the city by a man with a hat. There he learns that: "Dios se hacía cada vez más grande y el hombre se parecía cada vez mas a Dios. [God became greater every time and man became every time more like God.]" p. 19.

The pompous style of this story will certainly not appeal to young readers.

nr   Arias Borrego, Miguel. Cuentos y poemas. (Caracas: Gráficas Herpa, 1980? 159 p.) Gr. 6-8.

The author wrote Parts I and II of this collection of two stories and fifteen poems "to affirm on a solid basis the good behavior of future citizens. " Thus in these stories and poems he admonishes young readers to personally excel and to love their country above anything else. In addition he teaches them about conservation: "Nunca se debe destruir un árbol. [A tree must never be destroyed.]" p. 20. The melodramatic poems deal with one's native country, a friend, a soldier, God, a bull, and other incredibly pompous topics. The third part represents young winners of a contest of children's literature. So, in the same style, youngsters from first (?) through sixth grade wrote about the exemplary life of Simón Bolívar, the greatness of mothers, the evilness of alcoholism, and other important topics.

One would hope that young readers in Venezuela and elsewhere will not be exposed to these wearisome, moralistic writings.

nr   Armas, Edda, collected by.   El sol cambia de casa.
      (Caracas: Fundarte, 1979.   135 p.)   Gr. 3-6.

         According to Ms. Armas, these texts are spontane-
      ous expressions of children aged four to twelve. It in-
      cludes original stories written by children, stories nar-
      rated by children, and stories narrated and illustrated by
      children. The artistic expression of children is indeed
      a marvelous endeavor, but to believe that other children
      will enjoy reading these one-paragraph "stories" is a
      ludicrous and wasteful effort.

nr   Espinoza, Jesus Salvador Castillo, and others.   Caminos
      de papel.   Illus: Luis Beltran Caraballo and others.
      (Caracas: Concejo Municipal del Distrito Federal, 1979.
      40 p.)   Gr. 5-8.

         The editors collected these stories so that young
      readers would appreciate the life and customs of Vene-
      zuela.   The result is twelve stilted stories about a kind
      policeman, a school party, two brothers, a fishing trip,
      and others which probably will not stimulate young read-
      ers "to learn or to build a more kind and generous
      world. "   The illustrations are as rigid as the stories.

nr   Hedderich, Hernán.   Trece cuentos para niños de ayer
      y de hoy.   (Caracas: Hernán Hedderich, 1979.   103 p.)
      Gr. 7-9.

         These thirteen righteous stories emphasize the suf-
      fering and poverty of the farmers of Venezuela, the in-
      equities among men, the slavery of black people, the
      loss of property of the Indians, and how all of this could
      be overcome if everybody lived in "open brotherhood lov-
      ing intensely the warm countryside of Venezuela. "   Spir-
      itless black-and-white illustrations complement these
      slow-moving stories.

m   Paz Castillo, Fernando.   El príncipe moro.   Illus:
      Vicky Sempere.   (Caracas: Ediciones Ekaré, 1978.
      [34 p.])   Gr. 2-4.

         There are bland, two-tone illustrations and simple
      rhymes in this book, which tells the story of a Moorish

prince who twice lost his kingdom through the deceit of
a wicked fairy.   The small size of this book (6" x 6")
might appeal to some readers; however, it also limits
its usefulness in a library setting.

*   Pipo Kilómetro viaja por Venezuela.   Primera parte.
     (Caracas: Cromotip, 1980? [40 p.]) Gr. 3-5.

     Pipo, a young Venezuelan boy, embarks on an imag-
inary trip to see his country.   A simple text and pleasing watercolor illustrations show Pipo flying on a kite
over Maracaibo; arriving at the port of La Guaira; wak-
ing up in Pertigalete, where there is a huge cement factory; walking on the streets of Caracas, the capital, with
its traffic and pollution; and visiting mountains, valleys,
and small towns of Venezuela.   (This story continues in
Part II, below.) There is a simple map of Venezuela on
the last page of this volume.   This is certainly a most
appealing introduction to the geography of Venezuela.

*   Pipo Kilómetro viaja por Venezuela.   Segunda parte.
     (Caracas: Cromotip, 1980? [34 p.]) Gr. 3-5.

     Pipo continues on his imaginary trip through Venezuela
(see entry above).   This time he goes by vast forests;
beautiful fields; the great Orinoco River; huge dams that
produce electricity; and Salto Angel, the world's highest
waterfall.   He also meets two Indians who help him
cross the river in a canoe, and he sees a few animals--
herons and turtles--that inhabit Venezuela.   As in Part
I, this volume also has a simple text and attractive watercolor illustrations.   As previously stated, this is a
most appealing introduction of the geography of Venezuela.

LEGENDS

*   Armellada, Fray Cesáreo de. El cocuyo y la mora.
     Adapted by Kurusa and Verónica Uribe. Illus: Amelie
     Areco. (Caracas: Ediciones Ekaré, 1978. [34 p.])
     Gr. 1-3.

     This charming folktale from Venezuela tells why fire-
flies are now black and emit light from their tails.   It
also explains that fireflies still court mulberry trees

when they are in bloom, as they are still waiting for
their love.   Pleasing, colorful illustrations complement
this entertaining tale.

*   . Panton ... (Una mano de cuentos de los indios pemón). (Caracas: Consucre, 1979. [54 p.]) Gr.
4-8.

Five beautiful legends of the Pemón Indians of Venezuela have been collected and translated into Spanish by
Armellada in this outstanding book with spectacular, colorful illustrations.   It includes the following: "Un rayo-
trueno herido, " which gives a vision of beings that live
in the clouds; "Un indio se fue tras una venadita, " which
tells how an Indian becomes a good hunter; "El indio
ayudador de una culebra, " which criticizes an Indian who
started a fire without adequate precautions; "Un indio
tragado por una boa, " which tells how a brave Indian
freed himself from a snake; and "El tigre inferior a la
rana, " which shows how a tiger was defeated by a frog.
The Pemón version of these legends is also included.
Perhaps the only flaw in this otherwise excellent collection is that the text is printed in very small size,
which makes it hard to read.

*   . El rabipelado burlado. Illus: Vicky Sem-
pere. (Caracas: Ediciones Ekaré, 1978. 32 p.) Gr.
1-3.

This amusing legend from the Pemón tribe from the
Guayana del Sur region of Venezuela tells why porcupines
eat roots, fruits, and seeds.   Lively animal illustrations
and a simple text describe hungry porcupine in his constant but unsuccessful search for food.   A brief introduction tells about the Pemón people of Venezuela.   Young
readers will need to be told that this tale uses the names
of the animals as they are known in Venezuela: "Rabipelado" for porcupine, "Trompetero" for trumpeter,
"Piapoco" for toucan, and "Poncha" for dove.

*   . El tigre y el rayo. Cuento de la tribu pemón.
Adaptado por Kurusa y Verónica Uribe. Illus: Aracelis
Ocante. (Caracas: Ediciones Ekaré-Banco del Libro,
1979. 22 p.) Gr. 1-3.

This excellent adaptation of a Pemón legend from Venezuela tells how a vain jaguar (Venezuelan tiger) was humiliated by humble lightning. A simple and readable text makes this story delightful reading for young children as they follow the jaguar in his early attempts to impress lightning, and then see how lightning can easily frighten the jaguar wherever he goes. The jaguar admits defeat and goes home. Colorful, bold illustrations beautifully complement the text.

m   Villafañe, Javier, ed. Los cuentos de Oliva Torres. (Mérida: Universidad de los Andes, 1978. 254 p.) Gr. 9-adult.

This collection of thirty-nine traditional stories and folk tales was published as narrated by Oliva Torres. Mrs. Torres, a humble peasant woman from Venezuela, never learned how to read or write; she learned these stories from her father. There is a great variety in these brief stories that tell about rich people and poor people, White of the Snows, an elegant thief, a liar chick, a father's advice to his son, a man who talked with death, and many others. All of these stories have maintained their original ingenuity, thus they are a true depiction of the folklore of Venezuela. They are, however, difficult to read or understand because of the vernacular, which sometimes does not flow smoothly.

m   _____, comp. La gallina que se volvió serpiente y otros cuentos que me contaron. (Mérida: Universidad de los Andes, 1977. 222 p.) Gr. 8-12.

These forty-six legends and stories were collected by Mr. Villafañe during his travels through various towns and cities of Venezuela. They are published as they were narrated by the common people of Venezuela, hence they are sometimes difficult to read. Due to the fact that these stories and legends have maintained their originality and fast pace, they are an enjoyable introduction to the folk traditions and beliefs of the people of Venezuela.

NONFICTION

m   Goldstein, Basha. Jugando entre gotas.... Text: Sylvia

Galván. Illus: Pedro Mancilla. (Caracas: Ediciones
de la Fundación Neumann, 1979. 46 p.) Gr. 3-6.

This story describes how water is used by human
beings, and the various changes that water goes through
in nature as well as through chemical treaments. It
emphasizes the importance of water in many aspects of
life. Inanimate illustrations do not add much interest to
the slow-moving text. (Some adults might object to three
of the illustrations: a child sitting on a toilet, a boy
urinating, a nude girl taking a shower.)

nr Hernández, Ana Teresa. Cartilla ambiental. (Caracas:
Imprenta Municipal, 1980? 40 p.) Gr. 4-6.

The purpose of this ABC is to foster in young readers the importance of conservation. Thus, it includes
brief paragraphs against cigarette smoking, throwing garbage, destroying nature, and positive statements urging
readers to love nature, maintain cleanliness, be courte-
ous, and other worthwhile reminders. Needless to say,
this ABC lacks reader appeal.

* El hombre y el dinero. (Caracas: Banco Unión, 1979.
48 p.) Gr. 9-12.

This is an excellent introduction to money and banking from a historical perspective. Through the use of
cartoons and a simple text, it describes man's early uses
of money, ancient Greece's influence on banking practices,
the Arabs' adoption of the decimal system in business
activities, the Chinese use of paper money, the first bank
in Holland in 1609, and modern banking services, including credit cards. The last eight pages tell the history of
Banco Unión of Venezuela with several kind words about
its services.

m Paúl, Luis Alberto. El petróleo: un encuentro con
nuestro destino. Illus: José Lovera. (Caracas: Oficina
Central de Información, 1975. 62 p.) Gr. 7-10.

The origin, historical uses, and present-day importance of oil are well explained in this simple publication
with amusing illustrations. It emphasizes the significance
of oil to Venezuela as well as the development of the oil

industry in that country.   The last seventeen pages
sound more like official government propaganda about the
"responsibility of the Venezuelan government in carefully
exploiting the richness of oil. "

POETRY

m   Barreto de Corro, Alicia. Viaje de la hormiga.   (Vene-
     zuela: San Juan de los Morros, 1977. 136 p.) Gr. 1-3.

　　　Twenty-four poems about ants at work and at play
and twenty-nine poems about flowers, clouds, clocks, butterflies, games, and other things common to children
make up this collection. Many of the poems are too abstract to be enjoyed by children; others are simple enough
that attractive illustrations would have made them much
more appealing to young readers.

nr   Castillo, Anibal. La rueda mágica. Illus: José E.
     Castillo. (Caracas: Ediciones en haa, 1980.   47 p.)
     Gr. 5-7.

　　　Included here are twenty presumptuous poems about
life, animals, robots, childhood, night, and other topics
which will not appeal to children because of their ornate
descriptions and affected messages.   The two-tone inanimate illustrations are as bad as the poems.

nr   Virginy Irazabal, Isabel. Menuda hierba. (Caracas:
     Corpoven, 1979. [80] p.) Gr. 5-8.

　　　This collection of poems pretends to foster in young
readers a love for school, their country, the geography
of Venezuela, work, music, animals, and mineral and
vegetable resources.   The overly sentimental style of
these poems and their obvious educational intent makes
them unappealing as well as dull.

RELIGIOUS STORIES

m   Darío, Rubén. Margarita. Illus: Monika Doppert.
     (Caracas: Ediciones Ekaré, 1979. [44 p.]) Gr. 2-5.

This is a religious story about a young princess,
Margarita, who was given a beautiful shining star by the
Lord. Her father, the king, who did not know who gave
it to her confronts her with the following rhyme:

> "¿No te he dicho
> que el azul no hay que tocar?
> ¡Qué locura! ¡Qué capricho!
> El Señor se va a enojar."

But the Lord comes to her rescue:

> "En mis campiñas
> esa rosa le ofrecí:
> son mis flores de las niñas
> que al soñar piensan en mí."

Insipid two-tone illustrations do not add much interest to Daríos' rhymes.

APPENDIX I:
BOOK DEALERS IN SPANISH-SPEAKING COUNTRIES

ARGENTINA

Fernando García Cambeiro
Cochabamba 244
1150 Buenos Aires, Argentina

CHILE

Herta Berenguer L.
Publicaciones
Casilla 16598, Correo 9
Santiago, Chile

COLOMBIA

Libros de Colombia y Latinoamérica
Apartado Aéreo 12053
Transversal 39 No. 124-30
Barrio El Batán
Bogotá, Colombia

COSTA RICA

Librería Lehmann, S. A.
Apdo. 10011
San José, Costa Rica

CUBA

Lucie Bolduc Inc.
505-38 Ave.
Lachine
Quebec H8T 2B9
Canada

ECUADOR

Sr. Jaime Jeremias
Libri Mundi
Juan Leon Mera, 851
Quito, Ecuador

MEXICO

Sra. Pilar S. de Gómez
P I G O M
Parque España 13-A
México 11, D. F.

PERU

E. Iturriaga and Cia, S. A.
Casilla 4640
Lima, Perú

PUERTO RICO

Thekes, Inc.
Plaza las Américas
Hato Rey, Puerto Rico   00918

SPAIN

Libros Talentum
Núñez de Balboa, 53
Madrid 1, España

URUGUAY

Barreiro y Ramos, S. A.
25 de Mayo 604
Casilla de Correo 15
Montevideo, Uruguay

VENEZUELA

Soberbia Cia
Edificio Dillon-Local 4 Este 2, no. 139
Puente Yanes a Tracabordo
Caracas 1010, Venezuela

APPENDIX II:
UNITED STATES BOOK DEALERS
(Specializing in Books in Spanish)

Bilingual Education Services
1607 Hope Street
South Pasadena, CA   91030

Bilingual Publications Co.
1966 Broadway
New York, NY   10023

Donars Spanish Books
P. O. Box 24
Loveland, CO   80537

Fondo Cultural Latino Ameri-
    cano
6621 Atlantic Blvd.
Bell, CA   90201

French and Spanish Book Corp.
115 Fifth Avenue
New York, NY   10003
        or
610 Fifth Avenue
New York, NY   10020
        or
652 South Olive Street
Los Angeles, CA   90014

Iaconi Book Imports
300 Pennsylvania Avenue
San Francisco, CA   94107

Lectorum Publications, Inc.
137 Fourteenth Street
New York, NY   10011

National Textbook Co.
8259 Niles Center Road
Skokie, IL   60077

SLUSA
88 Eastern Avenue
Somerville, NJ   08876

Eliseo Torres
440 Lafayette Street
New York, NY   10010

AUTHOR INDEX

TITLE INDEX

SUBJECT INDEX

142

COLORS
  Balzola, A.: Los colores 108
COMIC BOOKS, STRIPS, ETC.
  Mafalda: El televisor 65
CONDORS
  Movsichoff Zavala, P.: El cóndor de la vertiente: leyenda salasca 60
CONVENTS
  Perez-Lucas, M.: Teresa de Jesús cuenta su vida a los niños de hoy 109
CORDOBA (ARGENTINA)
  Mereb, J.: Tubito y la pandilla cordobesa 28
CORN
  Blackmore, V.: El maíz tiene color de oro: leyendas vegetales 66
  Urrutia, C.: El maíz 71
COUNTRY LIFE
  Armijo, C.: El Pampinoplas 81
  Baquedano, L.: Cinco panes de cebada 82
  Lopez, G.: Patio criollo 47
  Marval, C.: Los Quitilipis 27
  Urrutia, C.: El maíz 71
  Vega, A.: Pericón anda en las uvas 35
COURAGE
  Vallverdú, J.: El alcalde chatarra 101
COWHANDS
  Hernández, J.: El Martín Fierro para los niños 44
CREATION
  Hinojosa, F.: El sol, la luna y las estrellas: leyendas de la creación 68
CRICKETS
  Goldberg, M.: Corchito va por el mundo 18
CROCODILES
  García Sánchez, J.: El cocodrilo 88
CRUSADES
  Freda, R.: Los cruzados 15
CUBA--SOCIAL CONDITIONS
  Gonzales, O.: Nosotros los felices 57
CUBA--SOCIAL LIFE AND CUSTOMS
  Gonzales, O.: Nosotros los felices 57
CURIOSITY
  Almeida, F.: La curiosidad premiada 117

DEATH
  Araujo, O.: El niño que llegó hasta el sol 118
DOGS

HOLIDAYS (see also Christmas)
Gorostiza, C.: Los días de fiesta 19
HORROR STORIES
Hinojosa, F.: La vieja que comía gente: leyendas de
espantos 67
HOSPITALS
Capdevila, J.: Nico y Ana quieren ser médicos 85
Martín, S.: Yo quiero ser campéon 27
Puncel, M.: Cuando sea mayor seré enfermera 98
HUNTING
Sierra L Fabra, J.: El cazador 100

IMAGINATION
Canela Garayoa, M.: Utinghami, el rey de la niebla 83
INCA INDIANS, PERU
De la Jara, V.: Historia del antiguo Perú escrita para
niños 72
INDIA
Kurtz, C.: Oscar, Buna y el rajá 91
Osorio, M.: El último elefante blanco 96
INDIANS OF ARGENTINA--FICTION
Rubio, G.: Pichi Nahuel: pequeño tigre mapuche 33
INDIANS OF ARGENTINA--LEGENDS
Garrido de Rodriguez, N.: Leyendas argentinas 37
Martínez, P.: Leyendas argentinas 38
Yali: Las trampas del Curupí y otras leyendas 40
INDIANS OF ARGENTINA--SOCIAL LIFE AND CUSTOMS
Saraví, L.: Los eternos pibes 33
INDIANS OF ECUADOR--LEGENDS
Movsichoff Zavala, P.: El cóndor de la vertiente: leyen-
da salasca 60
Yuguilema L, A.: Cuentos y leyendas de mi tierra 61
INDIANS OF ECUADOR--SOCIAL CONDITIONS
Icaza, J.: Huasipungo para niños 59
INDIANS OF MEXICO--LEGENDS
Cook de Leonard, C.: Los gemelos contra los gigantes
67
Hinojosa, F.: El sol, la luna y las estrellas: leyendas
de la creación 68
INSECTS (see also specific insects, e. g., Ants, Beetles,
Butterflies, Fireflies)
Bressano de Alonso, O.: La abejita hacendosa y otros
cuentos 6

JAGUARS